Praise for Barlett & Steele

"Essential reading to anyone trying to make sense of our country's current malaise."
—*L.A. Times*

"Barlett and Steele are superb researchers and clear writers."
—*USA Today*

"Barlett and Steele . . . have some intelligent things to say about the unfairness and impenetrability of the American tax code, which favors the wealthy and allows dangerous accounting for corporate pension liabilities. . . . The book is strongest, and most useful, when it recounts the poignant stories of workers left out in the cold, chilling examples of exactly how far members of the middle class have fallen. The book will undoubtedly make you angry."
—*New York Times Book Review*

"The avuncular pair, renowned for chillingly accurate, if uncomfortable, observations, have meticulously sharpened their analysis. . . . Given the power of their past groundbreaking work on health care, the economy, and other political hot potatoes that shape how all Americans live, *Betrayal [of the American Dream]* merits a careful read from anyone concerned about the nation's economic future. It is almost haunting."
—*Associated Press*

"A brawling, journalistic mix-it-up. . . . The authors' passion and anger are as clear in these pages as they are in the title."
—*Washington Post*

"These guys are the gold standard."
—Graydon Carter, *Vanity Fair*

"Especially poignant in the wake of the Great Recession that officially ended in June 2009 but has barely abated for countless millions of U.S. residents. . . . Using memorable anecdotes gleaned from deep reporting, Barlett and Steele show how the ruling class has instituted policies that mean the near abandonment in the job market for returning military veterans who fought in Afghanistan and Iraq."

—*USA Today*

"Rich in detail about how we got into this crisis and provide[s] roadmaps out."

—*Seattle Times*

"Barlett and Steele address key elements of this betrayal [of the middle class] (globalization, outsourcing, taxes, pensions, financial-sector dominance), then offer suggestions for reversing it, including progressive tax reform, fair trade, infrastructure investment, focused retraining, and criminal prosecution of white-collar criminals. Expect demand."

—*Booklist*, starred review

"The dedication reveals the emotional heart of their enterprise: Not merely number-crunching chroniclers of middle-class decline, they are invested in the fate of the people who exemplify it. Barlett and Steele's preeminent talent is their knack for combining the micro and the macro. They look systemically at issues and policies, from the US tax code to healthcare. . . . Their conclusions are buttressed by details gleaned from public records. But they also use the paper trail to track down the system's apparent victims . . . the laid-off, the discarded, the pensionless, and the uninsured."

—*Columbia Journalism Review*

"Urgent reading for anyone interested in contemporary America, not least as [a] stark reminder . . . of what is barely being discussed in the presidential election."

—*Irish Times*

"The ostensibly willful destruction of the American middle class is laid bare in this villains and underdogs story from the Pulitzer Prize–winning reporting duo . . . for folks bowled over by the recent financial meltdown, Barlett and Steele's book will resonate."

—*Publishers Weekly*

"Donald L. Barlett and James B. Steele are continuing the crusade to save the American middle class that they began two decades ago as star investigative reporters at *The Philadelphia Inquirer*. . . . At a time when the future of investigative reporting is at risk in the digital reconstruction of American news media, Barlett and Steele could once again pioneer new ways of doing it . . . the publication of *The Betrayal of the American Dream* . . . injects a provocative populist imperative into an increasingly intense and perhaps decisive partisan debate over the fate of the American middle class."

—Leonard Downie, *Philadelphia Inquirer*

"Barlett and Steele cover a lot of ground in this relatively short, fast-paced new book. Their straightforward, impassioned prose is filled with real-life stories of people who are losing their grip on the American Dream."

—*The Progressive*

"The book is packed with important information and examples of the damage wrought by policies that allow companies to, for instance, avoid taxes, profit from sending jobs overseas, and strip workers of their pensions. And it does the important work of making clear just how badly the deck is stacked against the 99 percent."

—*Daily Kos*

"If ever there were a time to pitch a national read-in, this is it. . . . The text we should all be reading is *The Betrayal of the American Dream*, by the reporting team of Donald L. Barlett and James B. Steele . . . the book is a nuanced and well-researched report on the crisis of the American middle class."

—Mary Sanchez, *Kansas City Star*

"*The Betrayal of the American Dream* is an angry book, denouncing the lies of corporate America and the elected officials it keeps on a leash woven from money."

—*Shepherd Express*

"A primer that should be read by all Americans who really want to understand problems in our job market and our economy . . . fascinating and readable."
    —*Charleston (WV) Gazette*

"*The Betrayal of the American Dream* is an outstanding explanation of what we've done wrong, with suggestions on how we can stem the flow of our nation's life blood and bring back good paying jobs that are the foundation of a rapidly disappearing middle class."
    —*HuntingtonNews.net*

"The team of Barlett and Steele have produced excellent journalism in the past, and they have done it again with *The Betrayal of the American Dream*, an analysis of the pain caused by the economic crisis for everyday people. This is a well written, readable book on the economic crisis and the thirty years of looting by corporate America that led to the crisis. . . . The authors . . . place human faces on the devastation being wrought in our economy, and the pain and suffering imposed on the many by the few."
    —*DailyKos*

"Essential reading if you want to understand how we got into this mess and how we can move out of it."
    —*Rogue Columnist*

"Thank God for writers who are able to show the effects of political decisions on ordinary Americans. Two of the very best are Donald R. Barlett and James B. Steele. . . . They shine again in their new book, *The Betrayal of the American Dream*, in which America's over-arching economic and political trends of the past thirty years are laid out clearly in intensely researched detail."
    —*Creative Loafing Charlotte*

THE **BETRAYAL** OF THE **AMERICAN DREAM**

THE **BETRAYAL** OF THE **AMERICAN DREAM**

☆ ☆ ☆ ☆ ☆

DONALD L. BARLETT
AND JAMES B. STEELE

PublicAffairs
New York

Published in the United States by PublicAffairs™,
a Member of the Perseus Books Group

Printed in the United States of America.

Book Design by Pauline Brown
Typeset in 12.5 point Adobe Garamond Pro

Library of Congress Cataloging-in-Publication Data
Barlett, Donald L.
   The betrayal of the American dream / Donald L. Barlett and James B. Steele.
      p.   cm.
   Includes bibliographical references and index.
   ISBN 978-1-58648-969-4 (hbk.)—ISBN 978-1-58648-970-0 (electronic)
—ISBN 978-1-61039-320-1 (paperback) 1. United States—Economic conditions—2009–
2. United States—Economic policy—2009– 3. Middle class—United States—Economic
conditions—21st century. 4. Working class—United States—Economic conditions—21st
century. I. Steele, James B. II. Title.

HC106.84.B37 2012
330.973—dc23

                                                                          2012012879

10 9 8 7 6 5 4 3 2 1

TO THE MEMORY OF JOY WHITEHOUSE

CONTENTS

PROLOGUE

The Betrayal of the American Dream is the story of how a small number of people in power have deliberately put in place policies that have enriched themselves while cutting the ground out from underneath America's greatest asset—its middle class.

Their actions, going back more than three decades, have relegated untold numbers of American men and women to the economic scrap heap—to lives of reduced earnings, chronic job insecurity, and a retirement with fewer and fewer benefits. Millions have lost their jobs. Others have lost their homes. Nearly all face an uncertain future. Astonishingly, this has been carried out in what is considered the world's greatest democracy, where the will of the people is supposed to prevail. It no longer does. America is now ruled by the few—the wealthy and the powerful who have become this country's ruling class.

This book tells how this has happened, who engineered the policies that are crippling the middle class, what the consequences will be if we fail to reverse course, and what must be done to restore the promise of the American dream.

We have been reporting and writing about middle-class America for many years. In our 1992 book *America: What Went Wrong?* we told the stories of people who were victims of an epidemic of corporate takeovers and buyouts in the 1980s. We warned that by squeezing the middle class, the nation was heading toward a two-class society dramatically imbalanced in favor of the wealthy. At the time, the plight of middle-class Americans victimized by corporate excess was dismissed by economists as nothing more than the result of a dynamic market economy in which some people lose jobs while others move into new jobs— "creative destruction," it was called. Soon, they said, the economy would create new opportunities and new jobs. We said, *Don't believe it.* What happened to the middle class in the 1980s and early 1990s wasn't just a blip, but part of a disturbing pattern: a shift by Washington away from policies that had built the American middle class and enabled successive generations to do better than their parents, in favor of policies that catered to Wall Street, corporate chieftains, and America's wealthiest citizens. We wrote:

> Popular wisdom has it that the worst has passed, that it was all an aberration called the 1980s. Popular wisdom is wrong. The declining fortunes of the middle class that began with the restructuring craze will continue through this decade and beyond.

Because of statements like that, we were accused of being alarmists. But in fact we grossly underestimated how much more difficult life would become for most Americans. The workers we wrote about in the 1990s were pioneers of a sort never before seen in the United States. Unlike middle-class Americans for more than three generations before them, for whom life progressively got better, they were heading *down* the economic ladder. They were the first substantial wave of what will be tens of millions of casualties—most likely well over 100 million—as Wall Street and the moneyed interests proceed unchecked to dismantle the structure that has sustained America's middle class, all with the assistance and blessing of Congress. The country that once offered so much to its people—like the GI Bill, which put millions of Americans through college—has begun to eat its own.

In this book, we describe areas where government action or indifference has taken its harshest toll. Some of the examples we dwell on, such as the deplorable working conditions in Apple's Chinese plants, may seem familiar. But their context and wider consequences are often overlooked. Apple is America's most profitable corporation. It is a signature innovator in a field—technology—that has for years been said to hold the promise of lucrative and long-term employment. Yet this innovative company has left most of its American workers behind. If the United States is unable to retain the benefits of a successful company like Apple and its potential to provide huge numbers of good jobs in this country for years to come, what does that say about our ability to encourage future innovators and provide employment here at home? Apple's phenomenal business success has benefited only a small share of the population, unlike some of our great corporations in the past that provided a solid middle-class living for generations of working Americans while also rewarding stockholders with handsome dividends. For its part, Apple decided to take the money and run. It is by no means alone, just the most visible. In fact, between 1999 and 2008, according to *Tax Notes,* the definitive tax publication, foreign affiliates of U.S. parent corporations increased their employment abroad by 2.4 million jobs, or 30 percent. During the same period, they slashed their employment in the United States by 1.9 million. If our largest and most successful corporations are no longer working for the shared benefit of American workers, then what is the future of the middle class?

The skewing of the tax code in favor of the rich is a subject we have written about for years. In this book, we tabulate the unprecedented riches the preferential tax law provisions have showered on the wealthy, and we explain why they will hollow out the middle class for years to come. The well-being of the majority of Americans is also coming under assault from U.S. policies having to do with trade, regulations, and benefits. In each of these areas, we address the broader context, drawing on decades of our own research and observations. It is the cumulative impact that has been so detrimental to the middle class. Yet most of the media cover these stories as if they were isolated events, devoid of a larger significance or pattern. Unfortunately, the significance is stark.

At a time when the federal government should be supporting its citizens by providing them with the tools to survive in a global economy, the government has abandoned them. It is exactly what members of the ruling class want. The last thing they want is an activist government—a government that behaves, let's say, the way China's does. Their attitude is "let the market sort it out." The market has been sorting, and it has tossed millions out of good-paying jobs. Now that same ruling class and its cheerleaders in Congress are pushing mightily for a balanced budget at any cost. If it happens, it will be secured mostly by taking more out of the pockets of working people, driving yet another nail into the middle-class coffin.

The economic elite have accomplished this by relentlessly pressing their advantage, an advantage that exists for the simplest of reasons: the rich buy influence. As the divide between them and everyone else has grown since the early 1970s, the wealthy have poured more and more money into lobbying and politics in order to control the agenda. Now the "one percent" is plowing untold millions into political contributions and lobbying, and every effort to try to reduce the influence of money in politics has been rebuffed. With the Supreme Court *Citizens United* ruling of January 21, 2010, the message was driven home to the middle class that politics had become slavishly addicted to the big bucks of the moneyed class and that the ability of average Americans to influence elected officials would be overwhelmed by that money. Now, for a price, the elite will select the candidates and bankroll the campaigns, and few politicians will be able to afford to give up the corporate dollars.

Who are the members of America's ruling class? We use the term to describe an amalgam of politicians and special interests who have succeeded in making life exponentially more comfortable for the already comfortable, while simultaneously lowering the quality of life for everyone else. The book details how they have done it. The chapters form a mosaic whose overall picture is clear: the ruling class is defined by its ability to move money beyond the reach of government supervision. This has been accomplished in various ways, but the most important is arguably the establishment of a belief that government has no business in business. This creed has no basis in fact and is widely disproved by the performance of other governments around the world. But not in America. Instead, we have created the world's newest financial aristocracy, a class that has successfully put itself beyond the reach of government constraint and can do pretty much whatever it wants in pursuit of its own personal gain. This, they like to tell us, is virtuous.

There are no Blue Book membership rosters of the new ruling class, no secret handshakes, no regularly scheduled meetings. Wealth alone does not get you a seat at the table; nor does your family tree, your academic credentials, or your job title, whether in a corporation, the government, or a think tank. What counts is your ability to advance the cause of the group. The membership is bipartisan. There are seats for Republicans and Democrats, as well as for institutions, including representatives of the mainstream media. In the most devastating financial collapse since the

Great Depression, when the news media accounts were studded
with doomsday scenarios, the ruling class made conscious decisions to rescue certain businesses while they shoved others off the
cliff. In the process, both Democratic and Republican administrations ditched the notion that all Americans should be treated
equally, that the playing field should be level for everyone. This
quaint concept has no standing in a plutocracy. Lacking a civic
or moral compass, it's a peer group without a purpose beyond its
own perpetuation with no mission except to wall in the money
within its ranks.

In contrast, we define the "middle class" strictly by income.
Most Americans, even those who are affluent, think of themselves
as middle-class. But economically they are not. We have defined
the heart of the middle class as those wage-earners who reported
overall incomes between $35,000 and $85,000 on their tax returns in 2009. Median household income that year was $50,599,
meaning that half of all Americans earned more than that and
half earned less. That figure has since fallen below $50,000 as the
United States went through its first full decade of declining incomes when adjusted for inflation. Only the poor and the middle
went down. The rich tracked sharply higher.

All told, there were 34 million individuals and families in the
$35,000 to $85,000 range who reported wage and salary income on their 2009 tax returns. They accounted for 30 percent
of the more than 116 million returns filed by working Americans.
By far the largest group with job income, 58 million individuals

and families, fell below our middle-class definition. The remaining 24 million tax return filers fell in the upper-middle, affluent, and rich classes. While the merely affluent 20 percent in the upper middle maintained their wealth, those at the very top of the income scale—the one percent—dramatically increased their wealth. An extended middle class would include people with incomes up to $115,000. While that may seem large to people living in many towns across the country, it would not be nearly so impressive for a family in an expensive city such as New York. At the same time, at the other end of the scale, a new definition of poor puts one in two Americans in that category. Census Bureau and academic statisticians are still refining the definitions that will make up the new American poor.

Men and women of every age and profession within the middle class have been affected by the policies championed by the ruling class, but the ones who may pay the highest price are the young—those in their twenties and thirties. For the next generation, the outlook is even bleaker. Many doors that were once open to high school graduates have slammed shut. Factory jobs that offered a way to maintain a comfortable lifestyle have disappeared at record rates, and nothing has come along to take their place. The reason the Apple example is so chilling is that Apple and companies like it were supposed to be the forward-looking option for a better-educated U.S. middle class. As we show, especially with regard to outsourcing, the promise that education is a gateway to solid middle-class well-being has also been retracted for many Americans.

Growing numbers of college graduates are hurting, unable to find jobs in this economy that match the skills for which they were trained. They had been assured that a college degree would be their ticket to a secure future. Now many of those with freshly minted degrees are working at jobs that require only a high school diploma, expecting to be in hock for much of their productive lives, or living in shared housing with parents or friends because they don't earn enough to pay their own way.

Veterans of the wars in Iraq and Afghanistan are especially disheartened by the lack of options. Volunteers at a veterans' service center in Cape Coral, Florida, recall a young Army veteran who served in Iraq and received a Bronze Star. After his discharge, he returned to the States, enrolled in college, and earned a bachelor's degree. He was then ready to enter the job market, but he told advisers at the veterans' center that "there was nothing out there." He believed that his only alternative was to reenlist, an option that will be less available as Defense cuts start to bite and staffing levels are reduced in all the armed services.

Many more areas of public policy affect the middle class but are beyond the scope of this book. For example, we do not discuss health care here in detail because of pending litigation and turmoil in Congress over threats to repeal President Barack Obama's health care law. But in our view, the most fundamental problem in health care won't be addressed anytime soon. The U.S. health care system is based on the misguided notion that the private market is the best way to provide care and coverage to Americans. We focused on it in our 2004 book *Critical Condition: How*

Health Care in America Became Big Business—and Bad Medicine.
In that work, we documented the failure of the market system to
deliver quality health care to everyone at an affordable price. The
market system didn't work then. It doesn't work now. It never
will. Yet ideologues are committed to foisting it off on an unsuspecting public, and key lawmakers and jurists are prepared to do
their bidding, even though when compared with other developed
countries, the United States has fewer hospital beds per capita,
fewer doctors per capita, and fewer nurses per capita. But the bottom line is this: U.S. citizens die younger than people in more
than two dozen other countries, many decidedly less developed,
largely as a result of inferior health care. What the existing American system does very nicely, however, is enrich a very few people
and favored corporations.

The private market experiment has failed, but even Obama's
health care bill still leaves most of the power in the health industry in the hands of private insurers. It is a mark of how effectively
the ruling class's propaganda machine has become in framing the
debate in America that this relatively benign piece of legislation
would be portrayed as a triumph of "socialism."

There is a reason why Washington has turned its back on average Americans. We are no longer the democracy we once were.
We have become a plutocracy in which the few enact programs
that promote their narrow interest at the expense of the many.
Ironically, it was Wall Street that disclosed the emergence of the
American plutocracy. As early as 2005, a global strategist at Citigroup, Ajay Kapur, and his colleagues coined the word "pluton-

omy." They used it in an internal report to describe any country with massive income and wealth inequality. Among those countries qualifying for the title: the United States. At the time, the top 1 percent of U.S. households controlled more than $16 trillion in wealth—more than all the wealth controlled by the bottom 90 percent of the households. In their view, there really was no "average consumer," just "the rich" and everyone else. Their thesis: "capitalists benefit disproportionately from globalization and the productivity boom, at the relative expense of labor," a conviction later confirmed by America's biggest crash since the Great Depression. The very rich recovered quite nicely. Most everyone else is still in the hole. Some in the middle and at the bottom, like the millions who lost their jobs, their homes, and their retirement savings, will never recover.

Today, it's not just Wall Street that discounts the significance of the great American middle class. In 2011, *AdAge,* the trade publication for the advertising industry, declared the era of mass affluence over in America, adding: "Simply put, a small plutocracy of wealthy elites drives a larger and larger share of total consumer spending and has outsize purchasing influence—particularly in categories such as technology, financial services, travel, automotive, apparel, and personal care." From now on, if you don't make $200,000, you don't count, according to the advertising industry.

Barring wholesale changes in public policy, the coming years will be grim for millions of American men and women. To be sure, there will be ups and downs in the economy, enabling the mainstream news media and cable television to proclaim from time to time that all is well, just as they did in the early 1990s. But the dismal fact is that for tens of millions of middle-class Americans, as well as for the working poor who hope to achieve that status, the American dream is over. As for the mantra heard ever since the 1950s—that children can expect to enjoy a better life than their parents—only the delusional believe it today.

This is a sea change in American life without modern parallel. Where once we were told, over and over, that anyone could move up the economic ladder, now that movement is, with some exceptions, down. If existing policies remain in place, all that will be left will be the upper end of what once was a thriving, broad-based middle class. Everyone else will be toiling on a treadmill. "Retirement" will join "pension" as an archaic term in the dictionary. And if those who write the economic rules continue to have their way, those terms will be joined by some others too. Having dismantled the economic support network that underpinned the world's largest middle class, the members of the ruling class have set their sights on another goal that, if achieved, would put the middle class in an even deeper hole: they are promoting "austerity" in government budgets and policies—cuts in programs such as Social Security and Medicare—for everyone but themselves.

Only once before in American history, the nineteenth-century era of the robber barons, has the financial aristocracy so dominated policy and finance. Only once before has there been such an astonishing concentration of wealth and power in an American oligarchy. This time it will be much harder to pull the country back from the brink.

What is happening to America's middle class is not inevitable. It's the direct result of government policy, and it can be changed by government action. Look no further than at what the governments of our trading partners do to protect their people and advance the interests of their country. We could do the same.

But the United States has taken a totally different route.

"Running the country like a business means everyone is expendable," says Christine Wright-Isak, a former advertising executive who teaches marketing at Florida Gulf Coast University. "Is that the kind of country we want?"

In the forty years that we have been researching and writing about issues that affect all of us, we have never been so concerned for the future of our country. The forces that are dismantling the American middle class are relentless.

America must stop sacrificing its greatest asset. Because, without a middle class, there isn't really an America.

CHAPTER 1

ASSAULT ON
THE MIDDLE CLASS

Her name was Barbara Joy Whitehouse, but everyone called her Joy, and after you met her you knew why.

She was sixty-nine, and though hobbled by ill health, her eyes sparkled and she wore a smile. A wisp of a woman who had probably never weighed a hundred pounds, she radiated dignity and resolve.

Joy lived in a small home in a community called Majestic Meadows, a mobile home park for seniors just outside Salt Lake City. In her backyard was a shed that was filled with used aluminum cans—soda cans, soup cans, and vegetable cans—that she had collected from neighbors or found alongside roadways.

Twice a month she took them to a recycler who paid her as much as $30 for her harvest of castoffs. When your fixed income is $942 a month, as hers was, an extra $30 here and there makes a big difference. After paying rent, utilities, and insurance, Joy was left with less than $40 a week to cover everything else. So the money from cans helped pay for groceries as well as her medical bills for the cancer and chronic lung disease she had battled for years.

"I eat a lot of soup," she said.

As a young woman, Joy never dreamed that her later years would be spent this way. She and her husband had raised four children in Montana, where he earned a good living as a long-haul truck driver. But in 1986 he was killed on the job in a highway accident attributed to faulty maintenance on his truck. It happened during a period when his company was struggling to survive the cutthroat pricing that Congress legislated when it deregulated the trucking industry. After her husband's death, Joy knew that her future would be tough, but she was confident that she could make ends meet. After all, the company had promised her a death benefit of $598 every two weeks for the rest of her life—a commitment she had in writing, one that was a matter of law.

She received the benefit payments for four years. Then the check bounced. A corporate-takeover artist, later sent to prison for ripping off a pension fund and committing other financial improprieties, had stripped the business and forced it into U.S. bankruptcy court. There the pension obligation was erased by members of Congress who had passed laws allowing employers the right to walk away from agreements with their employees. In a country that once prided itself on creating a level playing field for everyone, those same members of Congress preserved the right of executives in those same companies to keep all their compensation, and even to raise it substantially.

To support herself, Joy sold the couple's Montana home and moved to the Salt Lake City area, where she had family and friends. With her savings running out, she applied early for her husband's Social Security at a reduced rate. She needed every penny. For health reasons, she couldn't work. In addition to lung disease that kept her tethered to an oxygen tank part of the time, she'd been further weakened by battles with uterine and breast cancer.

Her children and other relatives offered to help with expenses, but Joy, fiercely independent, refused. Friends and neighbors pitched in to fill her shed with aluminum.

"You put your pride in your pocket, and you learn to help yourself," she said. "I save cans."

Joy's story may sound like an isolated case of bad luck, but in one respect she vividly demonstrates what many other middle-class Americans experience these days. Thanks to Washington, Wall Street, and the ruling class, our economic security has been taken away. The good-paying jobs that underpinned a way of life have been replaced by part-time or minimum-wage jobs, if there are jobs at all. As steady work disappears, more and more people work under contracts, wages go down, and of course some have no work at all. Benefits that middle-class Americans paid for through reduced wages, benefits that promised to make their lives more secure, have been canceled.

And the worst is yet to come, as the privileged and their associates in Congress prepare to initiate slash-and-burn policies, beginning in 2013, to balance the budget—largely on the backs of the working middle class. That's when people will learn that they are expected to work until at least the age of seventy, assuming that they can find employers willing to hire them at that age and that they are healthy enough to handle full-time employment. At the same time that the government is requiring people to work until they are seventy before retirement benefits are available to them, for most working people fifty is all too often the new sixty-five when it comes to employment opportunities for anyone who wants to do anything other than become a greeter at Walmart.

The ills of today's economy are explained away by the privileged as nothing more than ongoing fallout from the recent recession. All will be better, they insist, when the economy recovers. They said the same thing twenty years ago when they attributed the economic failings of the early 1990s to a recession. The recession was not why the middle class was declining then. Nor is it now. The causes are deeper. The joblessness, foreclosures, and implosion of retirement savings that came into sharp focus after this last recession are no more transitory today than they were in 1992. The attack on the middle class goes back long before that.

For decades Washington and Wall Street have been systematically rewriting the rules of the American economy to benefit the few at the expense of the many—putting in place policies that have steadily dismantled the foundation of America's middle class.

The future looks bleak for all but the richest Americans if these policies don't change.

Indeed, it's grimmer than Washington is saying.

A majority of the new jobs being created are at the bottom of the wage scale. And there are still not enough. We are in the fourth year of unemployment hovering above 8 percent. In April 2012, it was 8.2 percent, or 12.7 million men and women out of work. The last time we were in this situation was during the Great Depression. In 1982–1983, unemployment was above 9 percent for those two years, before dropping back into the 7 percent range. But the unemployment number the news media parrots is a Washington spin figure. The real number of people without work is north of 22 million. Think of it as the entire population of New York City and the surrounding suburbs, all looking for a job.

Begin with the basic unemployment figure of 12.7 million. Add to that the people who were working part-time because they could not find full-time jobs, or who were forced into working less: 7.7 million. Now unemployment is 20.4 million. Finally, toss in another 2.4 million people officially identified as "marginally attached to the labor force"—those who had looked for a job in the past year but not in the month before the federal survey, partly because they were discouraged. Grand total: 22.8 million in need of a job—or nearly double the official unemployment total.

These figures will take on new meaning in 2013, when Congress begins to mindlessly—and needlessly—wield a meat axe to government spending. Not that spending should be allowed to continue unchecked. There are many areas where it should be reduced. But the spending that should be curbed won't be. Rather, lawmakers will pretend, as they have for several years, that spending must be slashed to bring down the deficit. Even Social Security will be on the chopping block. So, too, health care. What they really mean is the ruling class is getting ready to squeeze working people even more.

The financial deregulation that enriched Wall Street and triggered the Great Recession was just the latest in a long series of moves by the economic elite to consolidate their control of the American economy. They have:

- Created a tax system that is heavily weighted against the middle class
- Deregulated sectors of the economy and in so doing killed jobs or lowered wages for employees across entire industries such as airlines and trucking
- Ignited in the financial sector a wildly speculative run-up in mortgage-backed securities of little value that imploded in the 2008–2009 recession
- Encouraged corporations to transfer jobs abroad and eliminate jobs in this country to bolster the value of stock, increase dividends, and boost executive compensation

- Enabled companies to eliminate positions and replace permanent employees with contract workers at lower pay and with no benefits
- Allowed multinational corporations to shelter profits overseas and avoid paying taxes on earnings that could be used to help stimulate jobs at home
- Forced 11 million people with mortgages that exceed the value of their homes to make monthly payments to the banks that caused the housing collapse—a debt they will never be able to pay off
- Refused to support the growth of new industries that could generate jobs for the future

Look upon all this as the end of a broad-based middle class in America.

MORE FOR THE FEW

Throughout its history, America has dazzled the world with the outsized fortunes of its entrepreneurs and industrial titans. But the heart and soul of our democracy has long been its middle class, a beacon of opportunity to the world. Entrance into America's middle class meant a good job, decent benefits, your own house. Maybe it wasn't a way to get rich, but at least it was a chance to have a good life. It attracted the brightest and the best to America, and our life, economy, and culture were immeasurably richer.

The optimism of the past has given way to raw fear—middle America worries over how to pay the bills, whether they can send their kids to college, whether they will ever be able to retire. The insecurity is rampant. "I'd say 99 percent of Americans are not sure they're going to have a job next year," says Tom Toner of West Chester, Pennsylvania, a former telecommunications industry manager and engineer who lost two jobs to downsizing and offshoring before trying to start his own business. His income is a fraction of what it once was.

How did this happen? Who decided to dismantle the American middle class?

Despite obligatory comments about the importance of the middle class and why it should be helped, America's ruling class doesn't really care. They've moved on, having successfully created through globalization a world where the middle classes in China and India offer them far more opportunities to get rich.

The chief executive officer of a global hedge fund made this clear to Reuters journalist Chrystia Freeland when he told her, as she later wrote in the *Atlantic,* that

> his firm's investment committee often discusses the question of who wins and who loses in today's economy. In a recent internal debate, he said, one of his senior colleagues had argued that the hollowing-out of the American middle class didn't really matter. "His point [the CEO explained] was that if the transformation of the world economy lifts

four people in China and India out of poverty and into the middle class, and meanwhile means one American drops out of the middle class, that's not such a bad trade."

The only problem is that no one told working Americans they were going to forfeit their future so that people in China, India, Brazil, and other developing countries could become part of a global middle class. In theory, this should not be a zero-sum game. But it is because Washington and corporate America have structured the rules that way.

No one disputes that globalization, no matter what policies the federal government might have adopted, would have eliminated jobs in certain industries in the United States as Asian, eastern European, and Latin American economies developed to replace that work. But where U.S. policy broke down was in failing to make that transition less traumatic for existing workforces and compel other nations to open their markets to U.S. exports to offset the losses at home.

At every step in the globalization process, the American middle class has been misled by corporate leaders, politicians, economists, and others in the economic elite. When blue-collar workers first began to lose jobs, white-collar workers were told that globalization wouldn't affect them—that jobs in the growing service sector would in fact be the wave of the future, replacing all those factory jobs shipped overseas. But the same forces that eviscerated plant workforces are spreading through white-collar ranks, from information technology to pharmaceutical research. Under the trade policies pursued by the U.S government, very few jobs are safe anymore.

The result is a huge transfer of wealth from the middle class to the wealthy in this country, as well as to workers in China, India, and other developing nations. No one wants to deny people in those countries the right to improve their lot, but the price of uplifting them has been borne almost entirely by American workers, while in this country the benefits have flowed almost exclusively to a wealthy super-elite. Globalization was peddled on the basis that it would benefit everyone in this country. It hasn't, and it won't as long as current policies prevail.

What has happened to the middle class—the shrinking middle-class share of America's wealth and middle-class workers' loss of good-paying jobs and secure retirement—is told by statistics drawn from decades of tax and economic data:

The "One-Percenters": America's richest citizens, the "one-percenters," would not become notorious until 2011. In 1996, when we first wrote about the "top one percenters," recognition of their existence was just emerging. Based on 1992 data, the one-percenters were all those who earned more than $190,000, with income going all the way up to millions of dollars. The average income of those at the top went up 215 percent from 1980 to 1992, compared to 67 percent for the bottom 90 percent of tax filers. By 2010 the baseline for the one percent was $344,000. A more revealing number was the *average* earnings of the top income group: $950,000. By contrast, average earnings for the bottom 90 percent, according to IRS data, came to $36,000.

Executive Excess: While earnings for middle-income wage-earners have been stagnant for decades, executive compensation has soared. In 1980 the average CEO was paid about 42 times more than the average factory worker. By 1990—when we were researching *America: What Went Wrong?*—CEO pay had climbed to more than 100 times that of average workers. Since then, it has tripled: today CEO pay is 325 times more than the pay of factory workers. If the earnings of manufacturing workers had gone up at the same rate as the compensation for corporate chiefs since 1990, factory workers today would earn on average $82,000. In fact, they take home about $40,000 a year, according to the Bureau of Labor Statistics (BLS). CEO pay is now so hefty that it often exceeds the corporation's annual federal tax bill.

Subsidizing the Rich: People generally understand the origin of the nation's deficit: we spend more money than we take in. But why do we take in so little? Statistics culled from the mountain of IRS personal tax data available show that in 1980 a total of 4,410 individuals and couples with adjusted gross income of $1 million up to tens of millions filed federal tax returns. On average, they reported that they owed $999,944—in other words, just short of $1 million each.

Now jump forward twenty-seven years to 2007, the peak year for the financial bubble. That year 18,394 individuals and couples filed tax returns listing adjusted gross income of more than

$10 million. Even adjusting for inflation, that represented a generous increase from 1980. Actually, it added up to about four times more money in real dollars. In any event, the average tax paid came to $6.0 million.

But the really telling numbers are these: The 1980 taxes paid averaged 47.9 percent of income. The 2007 taxes paid came to a meager 19.8 percent of income. If the nation's richest tax return filers had paid at the same rate as those twenty-seven years earlier, the U.S. Treasury would have taken in a whopping $157 billion a year in added revenue—or as the people who like to play with numbers in Washington would put it, $1.5 trillion over ten years. More to the point, $1.5 trillion never would have been added to the debt, and no interest payments on that amount would have been made.

Corporate Greed: One explanation for the tax burden on middle America is that for years U.S multinational corporations have refused to bring home billions of dollars they've earned on overseas sales because they don't want to pay taxes on those profits.

Sitting in banks in the Cayman Islands, the Bahamas, Switzerland, Luxembourg, Singapore, and other tax-friendly jurisdictions is a staggering amount of money—an estimated $2 trillion, a sum equal to all the money spent by all the states combined every year, or more than half the size of the annual federal budget.

The corporations say they will bring these overseas profits back to the United States to invest in the country and create jobs, but only if Congress wipes out nearly all the taxes they owe by reducing their rate from 35 percent to 5.25 percent. To appreciate the pure greed and arrogance of this stance, the next time you are required to send a check to the IRS to pay your personal income tax, imagine what would happen if you advised the agency that you will pay only a fraction of what you owe.

When corporations were given a similar tax break in 2004, they repatriated $312 billion and avoided taxes of $3.3 billion over ten years. But the program was a sham. Rather than create jobs, according to the U.S. Senate Subcommittee on Permanent Investigations, the proceeds from the tax holiday were used by multinational corporations to pay more to their executives and stockholders while they cut more jobs in the United States.

The fifteen corporations that brought back the most money reduced their U.S. workforces by 20,900. One of the most aggressive was Pfizer, the world's largest pharmaceutical company. Pfizer eliminated 11,700 jobs in the United States after celebrating the tax holiday. The company's CEO, Henry McKinnell, made out just fine during this period. While Pfizer was cutting jobs, McKinnell's compensation soared 72 percent in 2004, to $16.6 million. When he retired two years later, McKinnell walked off with a $200 million severance package, which included $305,644 for unused vacation days.

Entitlements for the One Percent: The federal budget deficit is a big issue with the wealthy and their think tanks. Typical of the position they espouse is that of Peter G. Peterson, the billionaire cofounder of the Blackstone Group, the big Wall Street private equity firm. Peterson says the deficit is a "real threat to America's future" and has the nation on an "unthinkable and unsustainable path." But how did this deficit get so out of control?

Peterson points to Social Security and Medicare as among the chief culprits in creating "trillions of dollars of entitlement obligations." But let's look at it another way.

Since 2001, tax cuts to the rich, including Peterson, have totaled $700 billion, according to IRS data. How did the federal government make up for the lost tax revenue? The Treasury issued more IOUs, adding $700 billion to the federal debt. Paying the interest on that debt in years to come will fall heaviest on the middle class.

Vanishing Jobs: Ever since jobs began to be exported from the United States, the elite have sought to assure Americans that the number was small and would not have a significant effect on overall employment. In 2007 Jacob Kirkegaard of the Peterson Institute for International Economics contended that concerns over offshoring had been "vastly overblown" and that only about 4 percent of those who had been laid off had lost their jobs because work was shipped offshore.

Financial writers picked up on the study to echo that theme. In a May 16, 2007, column, Robert J. Samuelson thundered: "Remember the great 'offshoring' debate? . . . Merciless multinational companies would find the cheapest labor and to heck with all the lives ruined in the process. What happened? Well, not much." Samuelson cited Kirkegaard in contending that offshoring was no big deal.

But offshoring is a huge deal. Samuelson, like other media cheerleaders, failed to take into account the trends already under way when he dismissed warnings about it. Although the U.S. Department of Labor does not have definitive statistics on the number of jobs sent offshore each year, a little-noticed report by the agency's economists in 2008 concluded that 160 service occupations employing 30 million Americans—more than 25 percent of the entire service industry workforce—were "susceptible to off shoring."

If the past is a guide, any job that can be offshored will be. An analysis by Princeton University economist Alan S. Blinder, using 2004 data to measure potential job losses in both the manufacturing and service industries, concluded that 291 occupations accounting for 38 million jobs—29 percent of the workforce—could be offshored.

RIGGING THE SYSTEM

For what has happened to jobs, retirement savings, and other vital signs of America's economic health, you can thank Congress and a succession of presidents who make the rules for the American economy. These rules determine the kind of job you may have, how much you will pay in taxes, and whether you have health benefits or a pension.

Congress makes the rules when it enacts new laws and amends or rescinds others—and then votes on whether or not to provide the resources that determine whether the laws will be enforced.

The president makes the rules through the departments and agencies that implement new regulations and amend or rescind others—and then either enforce or ignore these regulations.

Both the Congress and the president make the rules when they succumb to pressure from special interests and fail to enact laws or implement regulations that would level the economic playing field for everyone.

Taken together, the myriad laws and federal regulations form a set of rules that govern the way business operates—from trade to taxes, from regulatory oversight to bankruptcy, from health care to pensions, from corporate write-offs to investment practices.

In every era, these rules establish a system of rewards and penalties that influence business behavior, which in turn has a wide-ranging impact on your daily life:

- From the price you pay for a gallon of gasoline or a quart of milk to the elimination of your job
- From the cost of your favorite cereal to the size of your unemployment check if you've been laid off
- From whether the company you work for expands in the United States or shifts your job to Mexico
- From the size of your pension to the question of whether you will even have a pension

Ultimately, the rule-makers in Washington determine who, among the principal players in the U.S. economy, is most favored, who is simply ignored, and who is penalized. In the last few decades, the rules have been nearly universally weighted against working Americans.

That a huge wealth gap exists in this country is now so widely recognized and accepted as fact that most people have lost track of how it happened. One of the purposes of this book is to show how the gap became so huge and to explain why it was no accident.

Over the last four decades, the elite have systematically rewritten the rules to take care of themselves at everyone else's expense. As postwar U.S. history shows, it doesn't have to be this way. For decades after World War II, personal income in the United States grew at roughly the same rate for the rich and everyone else, all except for the poorest Americans. During this period, the gap between the rich and the middle class remained about the same.

The rich would have you believe that high taxes are a damper on the economy, but the postwar economic boom was marked by the highest personal income tax rates on the wealthy in peacetime U.S. history. At one point in the early 1950s, the top rate was 92 percent. No one actually paid 92 percent of their total income in taxes, but the wealthy paid a much higher percentage in taxes than they have paid for many years since. The federal government collected that tax money and routinely reinvested it in the American people. Veterans were able to go to college, families bought homes for the first time, and government invested in infrastructure projects such as the interstate highway system—

the benefits of which all Americans continue to enjoy to this day. All boats rose.

But in the 1970s things began to change. Middle-class incomes, after growing steadily for decades, began to flatten, while incomes in the top bracket rose by quantum leaps. By the early years of the twenty-first century, the rich had captured the lion's share of the nation's growing wealth. And they paid taxes at little more than a token rate.

From 2002 to 2007, the income gains of the top one percent rose 62 percent, compared to just 4 percent for the bottom 90 percent of households, according to economists Emmanuel Saez and Thomas Piketty. Consequently, by 2007 the top one percent of Americans claimed a larger share of the nation's income than at any time since 1928. Among the richest of the rich—individuals and families with incomes in the top one-tenth of one percent—the gains were even more astronomical: their income rose 94 percent, or $3.5 million a household, from 2002 to 2007, according to Saez and Piketty.

This, too, was no accident. The rich were getting richer thanks to public policy. Their greatest victory—one that would aggravate the nation's deficit and substantially widen the gulf that separated them from everyone else—was lobbying Congress to rewrite the tax code in their favor. Since the 1980s, with a few exceptions, the tax rate of the very rich has gone straight down and now bears no resemblance to the rate during the years when America as a whole prospered. The top rate on personal income—

92 percent—has shrunk to 35 percent. But that tells only part of the story.

In addition to lowering the overall rate for the rich, Congress in 2003 reduced the tax on income from corporate dividends, one of the key income streams for the very wealthy that significantly benefits only about 2 percent of taxpayers. In the 1950s, '60s, and '70s, millionaires might pay as much as 70 percent of their dividend income in taxes. In 2003 that rate dropped to 15 percent.

And they want more.

They plan to cut their taxes even further by having Congress eliminate the capital gains tax on sales of stock and other assets. During his 2012 presidential campaign, Republican candidate Newt Gingrich spoke for many of the elite when he proposed doing away with the capital gains tax, ostensibly to spur investment in America. Eliminating that tax would deepen the income and wealth gap and do nothing to create jobs in America. But that's okay with the folks who make the rules. In their view, inequity is a reasonable price to pay for the greater profit on the sale of, well, equities.

When word got out in the press in 2009 that Goldman Sachs was paying more than $16.7 billion in compensation, bonuses, and benefits to executives that year—in the midst of the recession—an outcry arose, but Brian Griffiths, an executive with Goldman Sachs International, brushed aside the criticism:

"We have to tolerate the inequality as a way to achieve greater prosperity and opportunity for all." *For all?* Griffiths was silent on when that "greater prosperity" might trickle down to the rest of us.

The economic elite are forever telling working Americans that the lag in their earnings is just the way it is going to be in a globalized economy. But other countries also compete head-on in the global economy—with different results. Germany and Japan have healthy trade surpluses, in contrast to the ballooning U.S. trade deficit, which cumulatively is nearing $10 trillion, far larger than that of any other country. That Germany and Japan provide education and training for workers is important, to be sure, but that's not why both countries are succeeding so well in the global marketplace. Germany and Japan are succeeding because each has national policies that protect basic industries and encourage jobs.

China is routinely the focus of our trade deficit. It rose from $84 billion in 2000 to an all-time high of $295 billion in 2011. U.S. government officials, lawmakers, and economists complain loudly about this, citing China's policy of manipulating its currency to keep the cost of its exports artificially low. But the problem isn't in China—the problem lies in us, and in our own policies.

Not so long ago, Japan was the target of similar complaints. Because of Japanese import barriers, American products weren't allowed into Japan. Over the years, the U.S. government repeatedly negotiated deals with Japan that were supposed to enable American companies to sell more products in Japan. But those deals were rarely enforced, and so the trade barriers remain.

In 1990, at the zenith of concern about Japan's unfair trade practices, the U.S. trade deficit with Japan was $41 billion. During the past decade, the annual deficit has often been double that. The Japanese are no doubt delighted to see America's anger over trade issues shift to China. It allows them do business as usual with the United States—to their advantage.

If the middle class has been hammered by U.S. trade policies that favor our trading partners more than our own citizens, it has also been hit by the actions of a group of opportunists at home who likewise benefit from favorable policies set down by Congress. These are the moguls of private equity. The activities of private equity companies burst into the national debate early in 2012 when Mitt Romney's Republican opponents (of all people) accused him of being a job-killer for his past work at the Boston private equity firm Bain Capital. Bain certainly did its share of cutting jobs at the companies it acquired, but there was nothing unusual about that. Eliminating jobs is what private equity funds do—all of them. This is how, for instance, Stephen A. Schwarzman, CEO and one of the founders of the Blackstone Group, the nation's largest private equity fund, has become one of America's richest men with an estimated net worth of $4.7 billion.

It's no coincidence that the private equity industry has exploded in the last two decades at exactly the same time that the decline of the middle class has been most pronounced. The money managed by these firms has skyrocketed, rising from $5 billion in 1980 to an estimated $1 trillion by 2012. In addition to 2,300 private equity firms, nearly 10,000 hedge funds, some of which are similar to private equity firms, have another $1 trillion under management. This means that Wall Street has $2 trillion in funds to buy and sell companies, often with disastrous results for almost all the people who work for them.

While the practices of many publicly held corporations have been detrimental to the welfare of their employees, the private equity firms have generally been much worse. Secretive, insular, and essentially unregulated, private equity funds have been free to pursue their rapacious job-killing strategies with abandon.

Typically, private equity firms borrow money to take over a company. Then they institute cutbacks and other "efficiencies" to groom the company for sale to new investors. When the company is taken public, the private equity firm earns substantial fees and passes on the debt it took on when it bought the company. Often the new company has difficulty managing the heavy debt load and reduces expenses by cutting even more jobs.

The list of companies whose employees were cast aside after their company was acquired by Blackstone is long and depressing. In what was the largest technology company buyout of its time, Blackstone in 2006 acquired Freescale, the huge maker of semiconductors based in Austin, Texas. Financed largely by debt, the $17.6 billion acquisition was a prelude to a string of job cuts of skilled workers. In 2009, again using borrowed money, Blackstone took over one of America's most venerable names in processed food, Birds Eye Foods. Blackstone instituted job cuts, axing the corporate staff of Birds Eye in Rochester, New York, and closing a processing plant in Fulton, New York, that had been a fixture of the town for a century.

To conservatives and free-market zealots, job cuts by private equity companies such as Blackstone and Bain, while causing pain, are absolutely essential and have a positive effect on the economy. Writing in the *New York Times* in 2012, columnist Ross Douthat argued that the "private equity revolution was necessary" and that "our economy became more efficient" as a result of often brutal restructurings. To Douthat and like-minded thinkers, the "competitiveness revolution," as he called it, has reinvigorated the economy.

But has it? It depends on what you mean by the economy.

There is no hard evidence that all this buying and selling has helped the economic welfare in communities across the country so that money flows from one enterprise to another, supporting other businesses and local services. What is absolutely certain is that the deal-making has been a boon to the bank accounts of Schwarzman and his fellow private equity moguls.

The managers of the largest equity and hedge funds have become immensely wealthy—many are billionaires—even though some of the companies they bought and sold later foundered. In addition to the rich fees they harvest, private equity fund managers rake in millions more courtesy of U.S. taxpayers. Thanks to Congress, a portion of their annual income is taxed at 15 percent (rather than 35 percent) under an obscure provision called "carried interest." This puts that income in the same tax bracket occupied by the janitors who clean their buildings. Using the proceeds from their deals and the money they save on taxes, private equity and hedge fund managers have lavish lifestyles featuring multiple residences, private planes, and ostentatious parties.

THOSE HIGH-PRICED AMERICAN WORKERS

The ruling class thinks that the average American earns too much money. This is an unspoken belief, and one that most of them would no doubt vehemently deny. But the evidence is compelling. The elite show their hand in many ways:

- When they oppose raising the pay of the lowest-paid workers, those covered by the minimum wage
- When they encourage the export of good-paying jobs in fields such as information technology
- When they resist changes in the tax code that would protect American workers

Corporate executives contend that they are forced to relocate their operations to low-wage havens to remain competitive. In other words, their domestic workers earn too much. Never mind that manufacturing wages are lower in the United States than in a dozen other developed countries.

Thanks to the rules, many of which are written by corporations, a company can pull up stakes and use cheap foreign labor to make the same product it once did in America. It no longer has to meet environmental standards. It no longer has to abide by U.S. labor laws. It no longer has to pay a decent wage. Then the company can ship the product back to the United States where, courtesy of the rules, it will pay little if any duty. How can American workers hope to compete against that? They can't.

Lisa Gentner worked at a company called Carrollton Specialty Products, housed in a one-story warehouse in Moberly, Missouri, a town of 15,000 in central Missouri. Carrollton was a subcontractor for Hallmark Cards, the global greeting card giant based 125 miles west in Kansas City, Missouri. The largely female workforce of 200 provided the hand assembly for a variety of Hallmark products. They tied bows and affixed them to valentines and anniversary greetings. They glued buttons, rhinestones, and pop-ups inside birthday cards. They made gift baskets.

As in many towns across the country, the plant was an economic anchor for Moberly. Manufacturing is often pictured as a big-city enterprise, but a substantial number of plants are the lifeblood of small to medium-sized cities.

Gentner started working on Carrollton's production line when the plant opened in 1995. She earned $4.25 an hour, or just under $10,000 a year based on a forty-hour workweek. She gradually took on more responsibilities. When a supervisor was out, she would fill in. When the plant manager was off-site, other employees came to her for help. She never had the title of assistant manager, but it was a role she often filled. A single mom raising three small children, she did nearly every job in the plant over time. "The best way I can describe myself was, I was a jack-of-all-trades and a master of quality," she said.

She had worked her way up to quality control manager in 2009 when Hallmark dropped a bombshell: the contract that had provided steady work for the women of Moberly for years was canceled and the work would be sent to China.

Gentner was earning less than $35,000 a year. By then, the pay of women on the production line had risen to just $7 an hour, essentially minimum wage, or less than $15,000 a year. But that was apparently too much for Hallmark Cards.

"We didn't earn a lot of money," Gentner said, but she was learning a lesson that many Americans have had to absorb in recent decades. "The heads of businesses are in it for what they can put in their pocket," she said, "and the less they can give me, the more they have in their pocket."

With jobs scarce in the Moberly area, Gentner did what so many who are thrown out of work do: she enrolled in school, the Moberly Area Community College. With the help of federal retraining funds, she studied business technologies with a goal of earning an associate's degree two years later. She had no idea whether she'd find a job, but she felt that if she had a grasp of business software she'd have a better chance.

"My theory was, if there are any businesses left in the United States, they're going to have an office," she said. "So it was job security."

On the eve of her graduation, the college offered her a full-time position in student services. That job, coupled with a temporary appointment to teach two night courses a week in Microsoft Office programs at the college, brought her income almost to where it had been nearly three years earlier.

Even though Gentner never expects to make back the money she lost after her job was sent to China, she feels that she's one of the luckier ones because many of her coworkers still have not found steady work. She's baffled by government reports indicating that the economy is improving. "I don't know where they live," she said.

In the Moberly area, as in many communities today, things are still rough. Good jobs are only becoming scarcer. As companies ship more and more work offshore, people who do find new jobs usually earn less than they once did.

"If it keeps up like this, within twenty to thirty years we're going to be like Africa," she said. "We're going to be living in little mud huts, drinking whatever water we can find floating across the road."

Lisa Gentner and her coworkers were put out of work not because the rest of the world's economy was catching up with America, but directly because of policies put into place by the powerful who rewrote the rules to serve their own interests.

They hired lobbyists and bought Congress to do their bidding, and they did something else that may have been even more important: they created a powerful propaganda machine.

The very rich have never liked the federal government, because it occasionally enacts broad programs such as Social Security, Medicare, and now health care reform that they regard as interfering with the private market. While that's long been their credo, during the last three decades they've acted aggressively to convert those beliefs into national policies by funding foundations and think tanks that agitate for lower taxes, smaller government, and less regulation—policies that benefit them. Authoritative-sounding research reports, studies, and news releases issued by these groups under the guise of scholarship are peddled to the media, receive wide distribution, and influence national policies on taxes, jobs, and benefits in ways that adversely affect the middle class. Among the super-rich, few have been more active and influential in shaping national policy for the elites than two brothers whose fortune is rooted in the plains of Kansas, and there's no sign that they think their task is anywhere near complete yet.

Charles and David Koch are two of the richest men in the world. *Forbes* calculates their net worth at $25 billion each, which, if combined, would rank them only behind Bill Gates on the list of richest Americans. They head Koch Industries, the second-largest private company in America with annual revenue of about $100 billion. They have holdings in oil refining, pipelines, and forest products, but the Kochs are also major investors in consumer products, from Brawny paper towels to Dixie cups.

The company was started by their father, Fred, who built oil refineries in Russia for Joseph Stalin before returning to the United States to build Koch into a profitable regional energy company based in Wichita, Kansas. He later helped found the right-wing John Birch Society and instilled in his sons a burning hatred of governments of all types. After his death in 1967, his sons took the company to new heights through expansion, acquisitions, and aggressive business practices.

Like many rich people, Charles and David Koch believe fervently in unrestricted free enterprise and as little government regulation as possible. But they aren't content to exchange their ideas with fellow plutocrats at their private clubs: they turn them into policy decisions that enrich themselves to the detriment of America's middle class.

The Kochs have contributed $12.7 million to candidates (91 percent Republican) since 1990 and spent more than $60 million on lobbying Washington in the last decade. But their greatest impact is the millions they have poured into foundations, think tanks, and front groups to mold public opinion in their favor by promoting positions that in almost every case benefit the few.

The rise of these conservative think tanks and foundations directly coincides with the economic decline of the middle class. Among the more prominent of these organizations are the Cato Institute, which Charles cofounded in 1974, and Americans for Prosperity, which David launched in 2004 as a successor to a similar group that he had helped found earlier called Citizens for a Sound Economy. Dozens of other groups receive Koch money at the national or regional level. In early 2012, a rift developed between the Kochs and Cato, sparking litigation by the Kochs and charges by Cato president Ed Crane that Charles Koch was trying to gain full control of the think tank to advance his "partisan agenda."

The environmental group Greenpeace, which in 2010 examined just one issue on the Kochs' agenda—their efforts to discredit scientific data about global warming—identified forty organizations to which the Koch foundations had contributed $24.9 million from 2005 to 2008 to fund what Greenpeace called a "climate denial machine."

The Investigative Reporting Workshop at American University has calculated that various Koch foundations contributed at least $143 million to more than two hundred groups in the three-year period 2007 to 2009. Many were colleges and cultural institutions, but others were think tanks and foundations. Based on its own research and information culled from other foundations, the Workshop estimated that the Koch foundations have contributed no less than $275 million to various groups since 1986.

One of the most significant, ongoing recipients of the Koch largesse is the Mercatus Center at George Mason University in Arlington, Virginia, just across the Potomac from Washington, D.C. Mercatus, which describes itself as "the world's premier university source for market-oriented ideas," has become one of the most powerful voices in the country for right-wing economic policy. It was founded in the 1970s by Richard Fink, a long-time Koch operative who heads the brother's multimillion-dollar operation in Washington. Charles serves on the Mercatus board, but the brothers' chief contribution has been money. The Investigative Reporting Workshop estimated that the Koch foundations gave Mercatus and its parent, George Mason University, $11.9 million in the years 2007 to 2009. Mercatus was one of the earliest and most strident opponents of President Obama's economic stimulus plan adopted early in 2009.

Interest groups supported by the Kochs spew out a steady stream of position papers, congressional testimony, and public pronouncements about public policies that are detrimental to the middle class. They back unrestricted free trade and oppose even the slightest government actions that might be interpreted as protectionist, a position that has helped destroy millions of domestic manufacturing jobs. They oppose any increase in the minimum wage. In 1970, before the Kochs and right-wing groups began railing about the evils of raising the minimum wage, it was $1.60. In 2012, it was $7.25, meaning the wages of those at the bottom have not even kept pace with inflation. Koch-funded groups have supported changes in bankruptcy law that make it much more difficult for average Americans to reorganize their finances when they are plunged into debt by medical bills or the loss of a job. That change has been especially harmful to women, usually single mothers, who for years have been the largest group of distressed Americans who file for bankruptcy.

The push by Koch-supported groups for the deregulation of industries such as airlines and trucking drove down wages and salaries in those fields and produced—in the case of financial deregulation—one of the most catastrophic financial bubbles in American history. Some of those groups contend that the housing crisis was caused by the federal government's wrongheaded moves to promote homeownership, while dismissing the much larger role played by Wall Street, banks, and the private equity market, all of which made billions bundling and peddling junk mortgage securities. Koch-funded groups agitate to cut Medicare and limit Social Security and would love to abolish both. In lieu of that, their goal is to privatize Social Security by turning average Americans' retirement savings over to Wall Street to invest in the stock market. Making Social Security benefits the equivalent of a 401(k) would further enrich stockbrokers but put most working people at even greater risk of poverty in their old age.

The Kochs are masters of misinformation. David Koch's Americans for Prosperity (AFP) virulently opposed the national health care reform bill and helped create the image that there was a vast groundswell of opposition to the measure by organizing town hall meetings to attack it. Speakers often made wild, sensational claims about the legislation: at one Colorado gathering sponsored by an AFP group, a speaker contended that the bill mandated physician-assisted suicide, charging that "Adolph Hitler issued six million end-of-life orders—he called his program 'the final solution.' I wonder what we're going to call ours?"

After the Patient Protection and Affordable Care Act (PPACA) was passed in 2010, the AFP bought television time on the eve of the 2010 midterm elections to condemn the new law. One featured a Canadian woman who warned about the perils of government-run health care systems. Identified on Koch's AFP website as Shona Holmes, she delivered an unsettling message: "Many Americans wonder what the new health care bill will do. Well, I know. I am a Canadian citizen. I had a brain tumor, but if I had waited for treatment in my government-run health care system, I'd be dead." She said she traveled to the United States for "world-class care that saved my life." An AFP official said that her case showed how "our health is too important to leave in the hands of a government bureaucrat." It was later revealed in the Canadian press that Shona Holmes did not have a brain tumor—only a cyst on her pituitary gland. The U.S. doctors who removed the cyst later said that they did not consider her condition life-threatening.

Similarly, the Koch-supported Cato Institute spreads misinformation about the economy. Every year Cato and its partners compile and publish an annual index of the nations that have the most "economic freedom." The most highly ranked have lower taxes, less government regulation, higher personal incomes, lower infant mortality rates, and fewer murders than those that supposedly restrict economic freedom. The survey is trotted out annually by Cato and other conservative think tanks with claims attesting to its scrupulous methodology, but its conclusions are based more on ideology than on science. Cato claims that nations that are "economically free out-perform non-free nations" but glosses over the fact that most of the so-called non-free nations, such as the Congo, have been poor for centuries and owe their lowly status more to ingrained poverty than current government policies.

Even more misleading is Cato's measure of economic freedom among developed nations. The United States is always in the top ten, but Germany, which has a dynamic, job-creating economy, always ranks well down the list largely because it has higher taxes and more regulation than the United States. In 2010, for example, the United States was sixth, while Germany was ranked twenty-fourth.

But what is life like for people in each country? The infant mortality rate, cited by Cato as a mark of a nation's prosperity, is much higher in the United States than in Germany—5.98 per 1,000 births compared to 3.51 in Germany. The murder rate, another Cato bellwether of economic freedom, is more than five times higher in the United States than in Germany at 4.6 homicides per 100,000 persons compared to 0.8 in Germany. German manufacturing workers earn 26 percent more in wages and benefits than their counterparts in the United States. Germany's unemployment rate in 2010 was 7.2 percent; in the United States it was 9.6 percent. German CEOs, on the other hand, earn on average about half what their counterparts in the United States earn, and then pay higher taxes on those earnings.

By most every significant economic measure, Germany's policies benefit the broader society. But in Cato's view, those very
policies—higher wages for working people, higher taxes on the
wealthy, regulations on corporations—are constraints on economic freedom. But whose freedom? To Cato, "economic freedom" is measured largely by how much freedom members of the
economic elite enjoy—not the freedom enjoyed by the society as
a whole.

The vision of the Kochs and members of the economic elite
for transforming America is by no means complete. The assault
on the middle class that we detail in this chapter is just a prel-
ude to actions that will further tighten the screws on working
Americans if the privileged continue to set policy that favors
only themselves.

To carry out their vision, the Kochs not only continue to
pump money into politics and think tanks but are aggressively
launching vehicles they directly control, such as the Americans
for Prosperity Foundation, which was founded in 2004. Although the brothers' combined net worth has risen over the last
three decades from $532 million in 1982 to $50 *billion,* they
decided in 2007 that the American dream—their version of it
anyway—was somehow under attack and needed defending. So
they launched what would become a regular conference, the "Defending the American Dream Summit."

This conference brings together hundreds of Koch supporters
who pledge support for the goals the brothers deem essential to

America's future. At a conference at a hotel in suburban Washington in 2009, David Koch thanked followers and said their efforts were succeeding "beyond our wildest dreams." Koch told them that meetings such as theirs were breathing life into the vision that he, his brother, and others have of creating a mass movement of Americans who will stand up and fight for the "freedoms that have made our nation the most prosperous society in history."

As Koch spoke, the gap between the richest Americans and everyone else had never been greater. The jobless rate was rising to 10.2 percent, the highest in twenty-six years. The number of Americans without health insurance hit a record high of 48.9 million. One in every seven Americans was in poverty. That month workers at companies such as Kasco in Atlanta, which made band saws and grinder knives, watched helplessly as their jobs were shipped off to Mexico. Only days before Koch's speech about the "most prosperous society," Heather Newnam shot herself to death as sheriff's deputies closed in to evict her from her foreclosed home in Tamarac, Florida. She was one of 332,292 Americans to lose their homes that month.

But those events taking place across America might as well have been happening on Mars for all those gathered in the conference room cared. David Koch told them that if they all worked together they'd preserve the principles that had made America great. "The American dream," he said, "of free enterprise and capitalism is alive and well."

What Koch didn't say is that free enterprise doesn't offer everyone the same opportunities if policies undercut members of what once was the world's greatest middle class.

The year David Koch launched the "Defending the American Dream Summit," Joy Whitehouse's dreams came to an end. Barely able to afford minimal medical care and enough food to stay alive, she continued to maintain her independence by practicing free enterprise as best she could—collecting empty cans by the side of the road until her strength gave out and she died.

CHAPTER 2

THE COST
OF
FREE TRADE

June 1979 was like any other month at the Rubbermaid plant in Wooster, Ohio. Out on the factory floor, huge quantities of plastic were being fed into massive injection molding machines, where it was melted down and then pressed into dozens of familiar shapes. Like clockwork, the big machines belched out storage bins, kitchen containers, wastebaskets, and other household products. Twenty-four hours a day the machines hissed and clamored, making staples for American homes—just as machines had been doing there for nearly half a century.

All across America it was much the same story inside busy factories that month. Orders for machine tools, a reliable barometer of the nation's industrial might, were up a robust 32 percent over the previous year, affirming the status of the United States as the world's greatest manufacturing power, the country where more cars, steel, airplanes, cameras, stoves, refrigerators, farm implements, textiles, and glassware were made than in any other country in the world.

A few weeks later, statisticians at the Bureau of Labor Statistics in Washington began compiling June's employment numbers from reports submitted by hundreds of thousands of workplaces across the nation. When all the numbers were in, BLS tabulated that manufacturing employment in the United States had reached 19,553,000 jobs in June—a new high. BLS took no special note. Employment fluctuates, and although the number of manufacturing jobs was expected to go up and down in the months to come, everyone assumed that in the long run the total would just continue to go up. It always had.

No one knew that June 1979 represented the zenith in manufacturing jobs, not a stepping-stone to greater things. Never again would so many Americans be employed in manufacturing.

National policies that had been undermining domestic manufacturing for years were finally catching up with workers on the factory floor. Years of low tariffs, unrestricted imports, and a refusal by a succession of administrations and Congresses to insist on reciprocal trade with our trading partners all began to take a harsh toll on the nation's manufacturing base after June 1979. That toll also went largely unnoticed, except by those who were directly affected. Unlike wars and natural disasters that capture the public's attention, the slow, steady erosion of the job base just wasn't headline news. But for millions of working Americans, it would be a cataclysmic event that demolished their standard of living and irrevocably changed their way of life.

Workers at the Rubbermaid plant in Wooster would live this story.

It was here in the 1920s that Rubbermaid engineered its famed rubber dust pans, an eminently practical item that became the first of many products that made Rubbermaid a household name. The company opened plants elsewhere, but the big gray stone building on Akron Road remained its heart and soul. Together with the company's nearby corporate staff, Rubbermaid's 1,600 employees made it the largest employer in the northeastern Ohio town of 24,000.

A good corporate citizen, Rubbermaid contributed to the arts, led a drive to refurbish an old movie theater into a cultural center, and sparked a downtown renaissance by opening a retail store on Market Street. It was perennially named one of America's finest companies and more than once snared *Fortune* magazine's top honors as "America's Most Admired Company." No one who worked the factory floor was getting rich. But it was steady work, and it was not uncommon to find three generations of a family on the payroll. Judy Bowman, who worked there for thirty-two years, recalled, "It was like a big family."

The forces eroding America's industrial base did not hit Rubbermaid in full until the 1990s. One of the most severe tests came in 1995 when the company lost a contract to supply Walmart with dozens of household items. Walmart, famous for squeezing suppliers for the lowest possible price and pressuring them to go offshore to keep costs down, balked at a proposed price hike from Rubbermaid. Rubbermaid had opened plants in Mexico, Korea, and Poland, but the bulk of its manufacturing was still in the United States. When negotiations failed, Walmart severed the relationship and turned to other suppliers, delivering a body blow to the company's U.S. manufacturing.

Later that year, Rubbermaid cut its workforce by 9 percent and closed nine facilities—the first significant retrenchment in its history. Four years later, the company was bought by Newell Corporation, a global consumer products giant known for cost-cutting and cutthroat management. Newell shifted work from Wooster's rubber division to Mexico and relocated the corporate staff to Atlanta. The Rubbermaid workforce in Wooster was reduced to less than 1,000.

None of the Wooster workers had any illusions about their new bosses, but even so, they were in for a shock. On December 10, 2003, Newell announced that the Wooster plant would be shut down within months. Shock and disbelief swept through the Rubbermaid community. Many employees had never worked anywhere else. All of them wondered what they would do.

Over the next few months, the plant was a scene of almost unbearable sadness to those who were left. "Little by little they took the machines out, one after another," Opal Drysdale, who worked in the plastics unit, told a local reporter. "All we could do was watch. It was really depressing; a big part of our lives was disappearing in front of us."

After the doors finally closed, workers soon exhausted their meager severance packages, and they struggled to find new employment. Some did, often just temporary jobs without benefits that paid 30 to 40 percent less than they'd been earning.

Judy Bowman had landed a job at Rubbermaid right out of high school. In the thirty-two years since, she had worked every shift, every day of the week; she had also worked almost every job, but mostly on the production line that made the popular rubber bath mats, until that work was sent to Mexico.

"I liked my job and I liked the people," Bowman said—so much so that the company called on her to lead guided tours of the plant for sales reps and visiting chamber of commerce types. She would show them how products were made by the big machines and then explain a little of the plant's history.

She was earning $13 an hour as a custodian in the plastics department when the plant closed. She was offered a job loading Rubbermaid products at the adjoining distribution center, but with nagging injuries from her years in the production line, she knew she wouldn't be able to do the heavy work required.

So for the first time in thirty-two years, she entered the job market. She answered an ad from the College of Wooster for a night custodian, but the college decided to use temps from a local agency. She applied to a new Hilton hotel to be a maid, but the job went to a woman with more experience. She applied for a custodian's job at a local hospital, but nothing came of that either. Months later she got a part-time job as a janitor at a local school district, working one or two days a week, for $7.77 an hour. As a full-time job, that would have added up to about $16,200 a year, slightly above the poverty level for a family of four.

The city of Wooster was shaken by the loss of its anchor company, but after the initial trauma the town tried to put its best foot forward, as towns are wont to do after the loss of a vital institution. Local officials said that Rubbermaid wasn't the only plant in town; there were others that could help pick up the slack. They pointed to other companies that could help ease the transition: LuK Inc., an auto parts supplier; Tekfor USA, an iron and steel forger; Bosch Rexroth, a hydraulic equipment maker; and Robin Industries, an auto components maker. But soon those plants would be shaken by the same forces that had destroyed Rubbermaid in Wooster: as companies began shipping work off to Mexico or relying on imports, workers were laid off.

In early 2010, the unemployment rate for Wayne County, Ohio, reached 11.1 percent. With tax revenues plummeting, Wooster-area agencies tightened their belts. The sheriff laid off thirteen deputies, demoted six sergeants to deputies, and cut the road patrol from twenty-one to twelve.

For Wooster's Rubbermaid workers, their manufacturing jobs had been a dependable way to earn a living, provide for their families, and spend their working lives in a hospitable workplace. The big stone building on the hill had been good to them—why else would so many of them have worked there for ten, twenty, even thirty years, often becoming the second or third generation of their families to do so?

But when the plant closed, few thought of seeking a manufacturing job elsewhere. Andrew Byers was just one of many who believed that within a few years Rubbermaid and other companies would be making everything overseas, then shipping back to the States. "There isn't going to be anything left but warehouses," he predicted.

The data bear him out. By 2011 the number of manufacturing jobs had fallen from 19.5 million in 1979 to 11.6 million— 7.9 million jobs had disappeared. More dramatic was the percentage of the total workforce that those jobs constituted. The good-paying jobs represented 18.2 percent of the workforce in 1979; by 2011 just 9 percent of U.S. jobs were in manufacturing.

So what did the Rubbermaid workers do?

Some took part-time jobs, some became temps, and others retired. Some, like Deb "Cuddles" Hoffman, trained for new jobs. Cuddles signed up to learn how to drive a school bus, a yearlong course of rigorous instruction in every facet of driving a school bus. There was no guarantee at the end that she would get a job, but she thought it was worth the gamble.

Why a bus driver?

"They can't eliminate the kids," she said. "They're not going to ship my kids to China."

OPENING THE DOOR TO IMPORTS

Across America, plants like Rubbermaid in Wooster have disappeared. You can see what remains of them in the abandoned factories that blot our cities and towns and in the novelties and collectibles that turn up in flea markets, products stamped MADE IN USA—flatware, toasters, cameras, eyeglasses, tools, toys, watches, jewelry, and dozens of other everyday items that are no longer made in the United States. Entire industries that were the backbone of America's economy are going or gone— shoes, apparel, textiles, machine tools, luggage, glassware, refrigerators, washing machines, air conditioners, cell phones, auto parts, luggage, printed circuit boards, televisions, and telecommunications equipment.

Many other industries have been crippled by Congresses and presidents who have turned a blind eye to unfair foreign trade practices that kill jobs and destroy companies. The once-vigorous American furniture industry, centered in North Carolina, has been devastated in the last decade by waves of imports subsidized by the Chinese government. The industry lost 70 percent of its production capacity from 2000 to 2010, and during this time nearly 300 plants employing thousands of workers closed. Imports accounted for only 19 percent of the domestic market in

1992; by 2009 the figure had risen to almost 70 percent. Another domestic industry, ceramic tile making, once boasted dozens of companies. Today only one major manufacturer is left: Summitville Tiles in Ohio. The company's president, David Johnson, told *Manufacturing & Technology News* that the "industry is just about finished."

And it's getting worse. The last decade alone saw the closing of 14 percent of the nation's factories (56,190 establishments), the sharpest industrial decline in American history. A record 5.7 million factory workers lost their jobs during this time. This 33 percent decline even exceeded manufacturing job losses during the Great Depression, according to Stephen Ezell, a manufacturing industry analyst. As those jobs have vanished, millions of middle-class Americans—whose income has stagnated or gone down—have struggled.

The decline of U.S. manufacturing isn't a new story. But what hasn't been told is how it happened, the role played by Wall Street and the ruling class, why it need not have played out the way it did, and why it symbolizes the end of an American era on the global stage. The demise of U.S. manufacturing dominance is usually pictured as the unavoidable result of the rest of the world catching up to the U.S. economy. But what doomed manufacturing jobs was largely an economic policy crafted by Washington and Wall Street that was sold to the country as a policy that would benefit the nation as a whole. Instead, the policy enriched a few at the expense of the many. They called it "free trade."

After the Second World War, the United States lowered tariffs on imports and thus opened its doors to manufactured products from abroad, in part to aid war-torn Europe and Asia. Because the United States was the world's richest nation, policymakers maintained that we could afford to lower trade barriers without risking any economic harm to our own citizens. How could a few trinkets and cheap transistor radios from Japan possibly hurt the great American economy? Plus, they contended, it would be good for the U.S. economy: the more other countries prospered by selling to us, the more they could buy from us, which in turn would create more jobs at home. Reciprocity with our trading partners, we were told, would make it all work.

Manufactured goods surged into the American market. The United States kept posting trade surpluses throughout the 1960s, but as imports continued to swell the surpluses dwindled—from $5 billion in 1960 to just $607 million in 1969. By 1972 a miniscule surplus had turned into a whopping $6.4 billion deficit. The U.S. market was open, but foreign markets for U.S. goods were not, and imports began to erode employment in long-established industries such as apparel, shoes, and textiles. The United States posted an anemic surplus in 1973 of $911 million, and that was the last trade surplus the country would ever see. Since then, there have been only deficits—for nearly forty consecutive years.

The term "trade deficit" may seem abstract, but a nation's trade balance is a fundamental indicator of the economic well-being of its workforce. When trade is in balance—when imports and exports are roughly the same—there are plenty of opportunities for good-paying jobs. But when imports swamp exports, as is the case in the United States, basic industries that provide solid support for middle-class Americans are undercut, and jobs vanish.

By the 1970s, it was clear that free trade wasn't going to be good for America's workers. The steady erosion of good-paying jobs was under way. In the beginning it affected only blue-collar workers in manufacturing, but eventually it would spread. All the forces were in play that would systematically undermine and depress the earnings of millions.

If Washington had been truly concerned about the livelihoods of working people, it could have dealt with the growing trade issue then and there by putting in place a system that was fair to all. Instead, it passed the Trade Act of 1974, which fostered the illusion that Washington cared but in fact ensured the continuation of the same policies that were destroying jobs.

The act was prompted after Congress held hearings on foreign trade practices that were hurting American manufacturers. It was the first of what would become a steady stream of trade bills in the next few decades. Sponsors claimed they were designed to safeguard domestic workers and force our trading partners to open their markets to American goods.

The Trade Act of 1974 was a huge bill filled with arcane provisions, but its main purpose was to show our trading partners that this country was no longer going to be Mr. Nice Guy. The act would be a template for Congress for decades to come—a sort of how-to guide to pacifying workers in the short term by promising action on trade, but doing nothing to solve the problem in the long run, thereby bowing to the wishes of Wall Street, which would make trillions on globalization.

In urging adoption of the 1974 act, Democratic senator Russell Long of Louisiana said that "the United States can no longer stand by and expose its markets, while other nations shelter their economies—often in violation of international agreements . . . [with] practices which effectively discriminate against U.S. trade and production." Republican senator William Roth of Delaware claimed, "This bill strengthens basic legislation and statutes designed to protect our industries from unfair or disruptive import competition."

The bill did nothing of the sort. Despite the new legislation, conditions worsened. The deficit in goods soared from $6 billion in 1974 to $34 billion in 1978, an increase of 467 percent. More industries came under intense pressure from imports, which threatened yet more jobs. That meant it was time for Congress to pass another trade bill. Lawmakers were scamming the American people once again.

This time they called it the Trade Agreements Act of 1979. While the title was slightly different, the speeches coming out of the Capitol sounded a great deal like the speeches that had praised the 1974 trade bill.

Democratic senator Daniel Patrick Moynihan of New York described the 1979 legislation as the most momentous trade act in half a century: "It begins a new era . . . that has one specific purpose above all: to see that non-tariff barriers to trade come down. . . . [And] to stop that hemorrhage of American jobs and industries profits."

Republican congressman Frank Horton of New York said the act "recognizes formally for the first time that unfair subsidies are damaging to international trade. It gives us power to strike back if a foreign nation harms our industry." Russell Long, who only five years earlier had given a ringing speech about the 1974 act's tough provisions, made similar claims for the 1979 law: "It will permit the United States to attack foreign barriers to our exports and it will provide more efficient defenses to unfairly traded imports."

Once again, misleading speeches were intended to pacify working folks and make them think that Washington was looking out for their best interests. In fact, lawmakers were looking out for their own best interests. Five years later, in 1984—as the goods deficit topped $100 billion for the first time—Congress returned to the get-tough warpath. Lawmakers railed about the unfairness of our trading partners, and they proposed remedies that they maintained would open foreign markets to American goods. In the Trade and Tariff Act of 1984, lawmakers asserted that they were beefing up the law to aid companies harmed by foreign trade practices.

In lauding the bill, Republican senator John Danforth of Missouri recited a script handed down from earlier debates. Danforth promised that the new law "significantly strengthens . . . that provision in the law which provides our government with the ability to retaliate against unfair practices against U.S. exports." Democratic senator Lloyd Bentsen of Texas praised the bill for setting the United States on a new course and scolded our trading partners: "The United States has taken the lead in building support for an open international trading system. The rest of the world, unfortunately, has not reciprocated. Our partners in trade have been quick to take advantage of our open markets while often managing to keep theirs closed or protected."

Three years later, the goods trade deficit soared to $160 billion, yet another record. Once more, sounding as though Congress was suffering from collective amnesia, lawmakers said that they were getting serious as they crafted the Omnibus Trade and Competitiveness Act of 1988. Republican representative Nancy Johnson of Connecticut called it a "tough trade law" providing real reform. "Its tough penalties include mandating retaliation when negotiated agreements are broken, compensation for parties that are injured by dumping," she said. Her Republican colleague Don Sundquist of Tennessee said that the bill would allow the United States to "go to our trading partners . . . [as] a strong, unified front against unfair foreign trade practices." Democratic representative William J. Coyne of Pennsylvania said that it gave the United States all the tools "we need to strengthen America's hand against unfair trade practices and start on the road toward reducing this enormous trade deficit." Democratic senator Bennett Johnston of Louisiana said that the trade law sent a forceful message to the rest of the world: "When the United States and its products are discriminated against by other countries, we are not going to take it lying down; we are going to do something about it."

It did no such thing. But that's because Congress's actions ensured that the country's workers would have to continue "to take it lying down." Five years later, another trade bill to open foreign markets was once again back before Congress. This was NAFTA (the North American Free Trade Agreement), a treaty that knitted together the economies of the United States, Mexico, and Canada by eliminating all tariffs among them to promote the free flow of goods. Even though U.S. manufacturers of autos, machinery, apparel, electronics, and many other products were sending a steady stream of jobs to Mexico, the United States was selling slightly more goods to Mexico than it bought, so in 1993 the United States had a relatively tiny trade surplus with Mexico of less than $2 billion.

Supporters seized on this to mount their most grandiose case ever: by lowering tariffs, NAFTA would be a bonanza for American exporters and provide high-paying jobs to U.S. workers. "We will have greater access to a rapidly expanding market that hungers for U.S. consumer products," contended a bullish Republican representative, Jim Kolbe of Arizona. But with millions of manufacturing jobs already lost and small businesses hurt by imports since the 1970s, many worried that NAFTA would accelerate the slide, and fierce opposition mounted against the trade pact.

Congress brushed aside concerns about jobs. "NAFTA will provide trade reforms that will lift all boats with a rising tide of prosperity," proclaimed Senator Orrin Hatch, the Utah Republican. "The United States will enforce its own domestic trade laws to deal with unfair trade practices." Democratic senator John Breaux of Louisiana predicted that American workers "will prosper and increase in numbers as a result of a free-trade agreement." In casting his vote for NAFTA on November 20, 1993, Republican senator Phil Gramm of Texas said that America would one day look back fondly on the day NAFTA was approved: "I think as we look back, people a decade from now will have a hard time understanding what was controversial about NAFTA."

Dead wrong. As usual, Gramm and the others were speaking for the super-rich ruling class and Wall Street. At the time, Gramm's wife, Wendy, was chairman of the Commodity Futures Trading Commission (CFTC) and President Reagan's "favorite economist." It was during her tenure that the CFTC exempted the trading of energy derivatives from regulation. When she left the CFTC, she took a seat on the Enron board of directors. Thanks in part to the unregulated derivatives, Enron collapsed, taking with it the jobs of thousands of employees and wiping out their retirement accounts. It was the canary in the coal mine for what would prove a few years later to be the largest economic failure since the Great Depression.

A decade after NAFTA's passage, the trade agreement was more controversial than ever. The claims of its supporters turned out to have been hollow, and the fears of its opponents came true. The much-vaunted trade surplus with Mexico that backers used to engineer NAFTA's passage quickly evaporated, replaced by a trade deficit that became the norm. The cumulative deficit with Mexico had ballooned to $698 billion by the end of 2011. Sometime in the next five years the total will approach $1 trillion, and another major milestone for American jobs deliberately terminated by the U.S. Congress will have been reached.

Rather than stimulate exports to Mexico, NAFTA triggered a rush of American companies to invest south of the border, and Mexican imports to the States surged. In the five years before NAFTA, Mexican imports increased 51 percent. In the five years afterward, they jumped 91 percent. General Motors even built housing there for its new workforce. Indeed, it felt almost as if entire portions of the U.S. economy had, as it were, gone south. As for exports to Mexico, the growth rate actually declined, according to the Washington-based Economic Policy Institute (EPI).

The numbers provided a warning of what was in store for American workers: In the five years before NAFTA, the United States maintained an average trade surplus of $168 million with Mexico. In the five years after, that number plunged in the other direction, to an average annual trade deficit of $12.5 billion.

After NAFTA, as companies large and small began shifting work to Mexico, the Labor Department was flooded with thousands of petitions from workers seeking unemployment benefits based on jobs lost through trade. Among them:

Woodward Governor Company, Stevens Point,
Wisconsin: 1,330 workers
Smith Corona Corporation, Cortland, New York:
874 workers
Oxford Industries, Dawson, Georgia: 340 workers
Sara Lee, Martinsville, Virginia: 300 workers
Key Tronic Corporation, Cheney, Washington:
277 workers
Johnson Controls, Bennington, Vermont:
276 workers
Emerson Electric Company, Logansport, Indiana:
200 workers
Alcatel Data Networks, Mount Laurel, New Jersey:
120 workers
Parker Hannifin, Berea, Kentucky:
114 workers

By 2011 an estimated 1.5 million American jobs had been eliminated by imports from Mexico, according to Economic Policy Institute calculations. EPI estimated that exports to Mexico supported 791,900 jobs in 2010, meaning a net loss of about

700,000 jobs. In 2004 EPI had estimated that lost wages from NAFTA job losses were costing American workers $7.6 billion a year. That's the equivalent of all the annual income of 150,000 American families.

To be fair, the fault lies not just with Congress. Every occupant of the White House, regardless of party, has been equally zealous in selling out workers on trade. For decades, every president has been an ardent advocate of unrestrained free trade and has resisted any significant step that might be interpreted as protectionist, even though our trading partners have been doing the opposite.

In 1976, when the U.S. shoe industry protested that it was being engulfed by cheap, government-supported imports from Brazil, President Gerald R. Ford refused to provide relief. Even though the U.S. International Trade Commission, itself a bastion of free-trade policies, had concluded that the American shoe industry was being harmed by Brazilian government policies that violated international trade law, Ford refused to side with the U.S. industry.

To impose tariffs on Brazilian shoes, he said, "would be contrary to U.S. policy of promoting the development of an open, nondiscriminatory and fair world economic system." Two years later, Democratic president Jimmy Carter also declined to impose tariffs on Brazilian imports. At the time of Ford's decision, the American shoe industry employed 172,000 workers. By 2012, fewer than 15,000 worked in the industry, according to the Labor Department.

In 1985, after thousands of textile industry jobs had been lost to imports, Congress passed legislation to impose higher tariffs on textile imports, but President Ronald Reagan vetoed the bill, calling it protectionist and a violation of free trade. "We want to open markets abroad, not close them at home," he said in a refrain that had become distressingly familiar to American workers in many industries. Even though he had just killed a bill that would have saved jobs, Reagan sought to assure textile employees that he was on their side and insisted that he would not "stand by and watch American workers lose their jobs because other nations do not play by the rules." In fact, that's exactly what he did. There were 746,000 textile industry workers in 1984 when Congress and Reagan took up the issue of textile tariffs. By the time he left office, the number was down to 728,000. In 2011, only an estimated 120,000 workers were left, according to the Labor Department.

NAFTA was negotiated under President George H. W. Bush, who pledged that the agreement would permit the United States to sell to Mexico "even more of the goods we're best at producing: computers, manufacturing equipment, high-tech and high-value products." But NAFTA was sold to Congress and the nation by Bill Clinton. "I believe that NAFTA will create a million jobs in the first five years of its impact," Clinton proclaimed on September 14, 1993. "NAFTA will generate these jobs by creating an export boom to Mexico." Clinton could not count any better than his predecessors.

During the George W. Bush administration, the U.S. International Trade Commission ruled in four cases that Chinese steel imports were unfairly harming U.S. businesses and workers and recommended that the president impose tariffs on Chinese goods. But in every case Bush declined to do so: "I find that the import relief would have an adverse impact on the United States economy clearly greater than the benefits of such action," Bush wrote in denying relief.

President Obama has given tentative approval for a plan to open U.S. highways to commercial trucks from Mexico, fulfilling one of NAFTA's promises. Every president since the first George Bush has supported the idea of allowing trucks from Mexico to deliver goods to the United States, a policy that would throw thousands of U.S. truckers out of business.

Who says that bipartisanship is dead in Washington? It's worked to perfection in trade policy—with devastating consequences for working Americans. Despite all the bluster out of Washington demanding fair trade policies by our trading partners, the United States hasn't had the political will to back up the rhetoric. To do that in all likelihood would require administering a dose of what the ardent free-traders call protectionism. Our trading partners know that's not going to happen. The pressure from powerful multinational corporations and the uproar from some economists and media personalities would make any move to establish trade restrictions—even temporarily—next to impossible.

So the charade goes on. While Washington mouths platitudes and gives lip service to trade reform in a never-ending cycle, the trade deficit soars. Thanks to both parties, the cumulative trade deficits since 1976 add up to a staggering $10 trillion. That's "trillion" with a T, an ocean of red ink that translates into millions of lost jobs. But you never hear about that. The politicians and the news media only talk about jobs created by exports. They never mention the jobs eliminated by imports.

OUR GREATEST EXPORT

On any given day, the huge gantry cranes at the port of Long Beach in California are busy hoisting bulk containers onto the decks of freighters bound for China. Inside these twenty-ton boxes the size of railcars are America's exports.

Politicians and economists have long hailed exports as America's economic future. Export jobs pay more than other jobs, they say. Exports help reduce the nation's trade deficit. And exports are a sign that America is competitive in the global economy.

So what's in those colorful containers stacked several stories high on the decks of these gigantic ships bound for China?

Scrap paper.

More containers leave U.S. ports loaded with old cardboard boxes, shredded documents, paper bags, and other paper scraps than any other product. "The U.S. has become to waste-paper what Saudi Arabia is to oil," the *Journal of Commerce* says. In

2010 an estimated 20 million tons of waste paper was shipped from U.S. ports. That filled a lot of containers, but it isn't worth much as an export. The total value of scrap-paper exports has recently been as high as $3 billion a year, according to the U.S. Census Bureau—less than 1 percent of the value of the $365 billion in merchandise the Chinese shipped to us in 2010.

Once they leave our ports, our old boxes and paper bags travel six thousand miles to China, where they are recycled into new boxes. These boxes are used to pack products made in China— toys, electronics, computers, clothing, shoes, furniture, tools, and countless other consumer goods that were once made in the United States. Then they're loaded into containers and shipped back to the United States, mostly to the ports of Long Beach and Los Angeles.

All this activity at our ports creates work. But what kind?

South Alameda Street in Long Beach is a busy four-lane roadway that slices through a district of warehouses, rail yards, and truck depots about ten minutes north of the port of Long Beach. It is the "Recycling Corridor," so named for its ragtag collection of businesses that recycle paper and scrap metal, another big export to China. At Corridor Recycling, the gates open at 6:00 AM, and pickup trucks piled high with old boxes begin streaming in. Drivers bring scraps scavenged from just about any place that has old cardboard boxes—shopping centers, supermarkets, retailers. They weigh in at a gatehouse, then dump their old boxes and other scrap paper into a mountain of refuse on the grounds.

On a good day, drivers say they can earn as much as $90—not the wages some once enjoyed when they held manufacturing jobs, but "for now," as one told a *Wall Street Journal* reporter in 2011, "this is a help."

The scrap paper is bundled into bales and packed into containers, then trucked to the port and loaded onto freighters. This creates some jobs for the recyclers, the brokers who arrange shipping, and the crane operators who load the containers. But it doesn't do much to lower the trade deficit or to provide good-paying jobs.

But there is a big winner. One company has come to dominate the scrap export market. It ships 225,000 containers of scrap paper from American ports, more than any other company. Its revenues have steadily risen as the demand for American scrap in China has soared. Probably only one person in a million would recognize the company's name—American Chung Nam—but anonymity suits the company just fine. American Chung Nam is the American branch of the global business empire of a wealthy Chinese investor, Cheung Yan, said to be one of the richest women in China.

Cheung Yan is worth at least $900 million, and before the global recession she was worth several times that, according to *Forbes*. She made her fortune largely by cornering the market on scrap-paper exports from the United States. She ships old cardboard boxes and other paper debris to her Chinese company, Nine Dragons Paper, which recycles the trash into boxes that

Walmart, Target, Home Depot, and other companies use to ship their Chinese-made products to the United States.

Founded in 1995, Nine Dragons is one of the largest paperboard producers in the world. Even with the downturn in the world economy, Nine Dragons had record revenues of $2 billion in 2011. The company has four modern plants in China, including one of the largest paper mills in the world—with plans for two more factories either under construction or in the works.

Cheung Yan's business is all over the world, but the heart of it remains the old boxes and scrap paper that unemployed Americans and others gather up and deliver to recycling centers in Long Beach and other U.S. cities.

But surely we export something of more value than scrap?

Yes indeed. On the list of our top ten exports compiled by the U.S. Commerce Department each year can be found automobiles, pharmaceutical products, and automotive parts. Those three categories accounted for $103.6 billion in exports in 2009. But imports of those same goods were more than double our exports—$209.6 billion. And that's been happening since the U.S. trade balance dipped into the red. Exports go up, but imports go up even more.

Which is why America has the highest trade deficit of any nation in the world.

As the trade gap widens in each decade, every administration in both parties has promoted the myth that exports will be the answer to job creation in the United States, while refusing to acknowledge the devastating logic of that claim: if exports help employment, then imports must help unemployment. Imports kill good-paying jobs at home, and we have been importing a lot. In 1980 we imported 7 percent more goods and services than we exported. In 1990 we imported 15 percent more. By 2000 the gap had shot up to 35 percent. And in 2008, before the global economy went south, it had risen to 38 percent.

Instead of admitting this, we talk about the exports:

Our booming export business . . . is growing four times as fast as the volume of imports. And much of this export surge is in manufacturing exports. Today industry after industry is finding itself in an export boom (Ronald Reagan, 1988).

Each additional billion dollars in exports creates nearly 20,000 new jobs here in the United States (George H. W. Bush, 1991).

Every time we sell $1 billion of American products and services overseas, we create about 20,000 jobs at home (Bill Clinton, 1993).

Jobs in exporting plants pay wages that average up to 18 percent more than jobs in non-exporting plants (George W. Bush, 2003).

We need to export more of our goods because the more products we make and sell to other countries, the more jobs we support right here in America (Barack Obama, 2010).

Many of America's fastest-growing exports in recent years are commodities you'd expect to see shipped from a Third World country: nuts, animal feeds, rice, oilseeds and food oils, sorghum, barley and oats.

There is only one category in which the nation is an undisputed export giant—civilian aircraft. But its days as an export powerhouse are numbered.

BOEING'S FAUSTIAN BARGAIN

The United States had a $43.6 billion trade surplus in civilian aircraft in 2010, when it exported $67 billion in passenger jets and imported $23.4 billion. Adjusted for inflation, that was about equal to the industry's trade surplus of twenty years earlier. In 1990, roughly 400,000 production workers were employed in the U.S. aerospace industry; in 2010 there were only 275,000. So even in an industry where the United States is said to enjoy a competitive advantage, we are losing jobs. Why? Like other multinationals, Boeing has been steadily moving work offshore.

To build its latest plane, the much-anticipated 787 Dreamliner, Boeing turned to suppliers in Sweden, Italy, South Korea, and China to make sections of the plane that previously would have been made in America by Boeing or domestic suppliers. Fully 70 percent of the Dreamliner is foreign content, according to the Society of Professional Engineering Employees in Aerospace, the union that represents Boeing engineers. In contrast, Boeing's 727 was originally built with about 2 percent foreign content.

Outsourcing is supposed to save money, but in Boeing's case it backfired. The Dreamliner came in at several billion dollars over budget and three years behind schedule before it made its first flight in late 2011. Many of the problems stemmed from Boeing's overreliance on a vast web of global suppliers, some of whom weren't up to the task. Some components were poorly made; others were missing crucial parts. There were problems with the environmental controls and electrical systems. Subcontractors who missed deadlines disrupted the production schedule for the entire plane.

"We gave work to people that had never really done this kind of technology before, and then we didn't provide the oversight that was necessary," Jim Albaugh, the company's commercial aviation chief, told a group of Seattle business students in 2011. "In hindsight, we spent a lot more money in trying to recover than we ever would have spent if we tried to keep many of the key technologies closer to Boeing." In other words, Boeing would have been better off had it done the work domestically.

Does this mean the company will bring jobs back to the States? Hardly.

The most unsettling thrust of Boeing's offshore strategy is the Faustian bargain Boeing has made with China.

China is buying more Boeing planes than any other country except the United States, and as a trade-off Boeing is shifting more and more of its aircraft production to China. Boeing has cut deals with China's largest state-owned aviation company, Aviation Industry Corporation of China (AVIC), to make parts for Boeing 737s, 747s, 767s, 777s, and now 787s at plants in China. Boeing officials say that more than six thousand Boeing planes worldwide use Chinese-made components.

For the Dreamliner, Chinese factories were, for the first time, the exclusive manufacturer of several crucial components, including the rudder, the wing-to-body parts, and the leading edge of the vertical fin. It's no wonder that when Boeing took the Dreamliner on its global introductory tour in the fall of 2011, the first stop was China. "There's no more fitting place to come than Beijing," Boeing executive Marc Allen told the press after the 787 touched down.

Boeing began shifting work to China years ago, but the pace is accelerating. As the company expands manufacturing there, Boeing is underwriting research and training, including a lab run by the Chinese Academy of Sciences, to explore the possibility of using more biofuels for jet fuel. The most ambitious research project to date was announced in 2011 by Boeing and the state-owned aircraft company AVIC to open a joint manufacturing innovation center (MIC) in Xi'an to increase China's "efficiency and capacity to supply high-quality parts of Boeing airplanes."

According to a Boeing press release, "the MIC, which will open in 2012, will provide classroom training for AVIC employees and hands-on training for workers in AVIC factories. The training will replicate Boeing's successful production methods for sustainable quality to strengthen AVIC's manufacturing and meet Boeing's quality, cost and delivery requirements."

Boeing and Chinese aviation officials maintain that the partnership benefits each party. Former Boeing China president, David Wang, says that China is now an "essential part" of Boeing's capability to manufacture first-class aircraft and that Chinese suppliers are gaining the know-how to do high-quality manufacturing. "So I think the interdependency means we must have continuous friendly relationship for both countries to succeed in the future," Wang says.

But will the partnership last?

At the same time it professes to be Boeing's partner, China is moving at full throttle to establish a civilian aircraft manufacturing industry of its own to build airplanes like those it now buys from Boeing. In 2008 the Chinese Communist government created the Commercial Aircraft Corporation of China Ltd. (COMAC), a wholly owned state enterprise, to "build a large Chinese passenger aircraft that will soon be soaring through the blue skies." Composed of domestic Chinese aircraft companies, some of which are Boeing partners, COMAC has already built a prototype, the C919, a narrow-body, single-aisle plane that closely resembles Boeing's 737—the bread-and-butter plane that accounts for more than half of Boeing's orders. COMAC has taken orders from Chinese airlines for 165 of these medium-range jets and plans to introduce them into service in 2016.

Even for the Chinese, with their incredible record of economic development in recent years, creating a civilian aircraft manufacturing industry in such a short time was no small feat.

But they had a lot of help. From Boeing.

When Boeing turned to China and other suppliers to make the 787's components, it not only gave them a lucrative contract but turned over to them the technical know-how for building planes—something the company had never before done.

"Before the 787," says Dick Nolan, a former Harvard Business School professor now at the University of Washington, "Boeing had retained almost total control of airplane design and provided suppliers precise engineering drawings for building parts. . . . The 787 program departed from this practice."

Nolan, writing in the *Harvard Business Review,* concluded that Boeing effectively gave China and other suppliers "a large part of its proprietary manual, 'How to Build a Commercial Airplane,' a book that its aeronautical engineers have been writing over the last 50 years or so." As a result, Nolan predicted, Boeing will face a "competitor from hell" that "will be different and tougher than anything Boeing has encountered to date."

And that's just the beginning. COMAC also has another passenger jet about to enter service, a regional jet called the ARJ21. Though not a direct competitor with Boeing's planes, the airplane provides more evidence of how quickly the Chinese are putting to use the technology and know-how that Boeing and other aircraft makers have turned over to them. In COMAC's view, the rapid emergence of this new industry shows the "political superiority of the socialist system which is capable of concentrating all of its resources in achieving great things."

Outwardly, Boeing doesn't express concern over China's plans to challenge the company in the civilian aircraft market, though company officials have said repeatedly that they expanded in China in part to be able to tap the fast-growing Chinese market for passenger planes. Industry analysts estimate that China will need more than four thousand new planes over the next two decades. On a visit to COMAC's Shanghai headquarters in 2011, Boeing's president, CEO, and chairman, James McNerney, was all smiles as he posed for photos with COMAC executives while holding a model of the C919 midrange passenger jet that is already taking orders away from Boeing.

At the end of 2011, Boeing had 160,000 employees, roughly the same number as in 1990. So at a time when the total U.S. workforce grew by 20 percent, Boeing's job force grew not at all. But that doesn't tell the full story. In 1997 Boeing merged with aircraft maker McDonnell Douglas, and when McDonnell Douglas's 60,000 former employees are counted, it's clear that Boeing's total employment fell sharply over the last two decades. Given the extent to which Boeing is building airplanes with parts manufactured offshore, the jobs that remain are vulnerable.

In contrast, the economic forecast couldn't look better at a modern Boeing plant in Tianjin, China, a historic port city southeast of Beijing. Boeing Tianjin Composites Company Ltd., a joint venture of Boeing and a Chinese government–owned corporation, manufactures components for every Boeing plane. The plant is expanding, and by 2013 the Tianjin workforce is expected to grow by 30 percent, thanks largely to Boeing.

To Boeing, Tianjin is a prime example of what the company has characterized as its "win-win collaboration" with China, a partnership that Boeing says accounts, either directly or indirectly, for 20,000 jobs in China. At the groundbreaking to expand the plant in Tianjin, Ray Conner, a Boeing vice president, told beaming Chinese officials: "We rely on our Chinese partners to produce high-quality components for Boeing airplanes, and we are excited to expand this successful joint venture to increase production and employment."

Rather than being the positive stimulus predicted by America's economic elite, the version of free trade practiced by Washington has progressively undermined the nation's economic future. Instead of supporting American workers and domestic industries, the approach that Washington and corporate America have advanced has left employees and small industries at the mercy of unscrupulous sweatshop operators abroad and opportunistic multinational corporations at home. The resulting loss in jobs and companies has been devastating. Congress has been giving away the store for forty years, and soon there'll be precious little left unless the policy changes.

CHAPTER 3

MADE IN AMERICA?

Innovation is the pride of America. But as we show in the following stories of two companies, the benefits of innovation can be squandered all too easily, and a venture whose success could benefit the entire country can be transformed into a corporate asset that rewards only the few who own or trade its shares. Unless the companies that innovate remain securely anchored within U.S. communities, no innovation, however inspired, can provide the basis for long-term economic growth.

In the last century, America routinely created new enterprises that did just that and provided millions of jobs—businesses that produced television sets, household appliances, toys, and hundreds of other products. These inventions were often the inspiration of young men and women who were fired with an idea and who brought their products to market through grit, hardship, and the help of dedicated coworkers, launching businesses that became job creators in the American economy for generations to come.

One of the countless products that came to symbolize American know-how and ingenuity originated in a Nebraska farm town of five hundred persons. DeWitt, Nebraska, one hundred miles southwest of Omaha, was home for eighty-four years to one of the most familiar tools to ever take its place in American homes. The product was the invention of a Danish immigrant, William Petersen, a blacksmith by trade and a tinkerer at heart who designed a pair of pliers with teeth that could be locked in place, freeing the user's hands for other tasks. He called his invention Vise-Grip. Petersen began producing the locking pliers in his shop in 1924 and sold them to local farmers and mechanics out of the trunk of his car.

The tool was an immediate success, and Petersen soon converted a defunct drugstore in DeWitt to a factory to produce Vise-Grips for sale nationally. The company weathered the Depression and prospered during World War II, when thousands of Vise-Grips were used by U.S. defense contractors, builders of Liberty cargo ships, and the British aircraft industry.

The tool was so popular that eventually Vise-Grip employed more people than DeWitt had residents. These were good jobs, with decent benefits and a Christmas bonus to round out the year, plus the possibility of near-lifetime employment and perhaps even a job for a son or daughter. William Petersen's sons and daughter followed him into the business and kept its family-run spirit alive. They helped employees with mortgages and would sometimes swallow increases in health insurance costs rather than pass them on to workers. It was hard work molding and stamping out the tools, but employees felt that they would always have a job as long as they worked hard. They knew that in tough times the family, confident that business would eventually rebound, would take less profit rather than lay them off.

Over and over in their annual reports, the Petersens stressed the debt they owed to their employees: "We want to say how highly we regard the people who make up this organization," the family said in a 1972 report. "It is their loyalty, industry, and skill which, over the years, have made it possible for this firm to grow . . . every job is an important job and every worker a valued and respected person." Generations of townspeople felt much like Linda Colgrove, who performed a variety of jobs at Vise-Grip in the nearly four decades she spent there: "You couldn't ask for a better place to work."

From this out-of-the-way village in rural Nebraska, Vise-Grips poured forth by the millions to supply the U.S. market and overseas customers as well. By the mid-1970s, more than 30 percent of the 7 million tools made in DeWitt were sold abroad. A decade later, the plant was making almost as many Vise-Grips for export as it had once made for U.S. consumers. Before economists and politicians began touting export jobs as a cure-all for America's job woes, Vise-Grip was ahead of the curve. Here was a unique product invented in the USA, manufactured in the USA, and shipped around the globe from the USA. It was a perfect template to map out America's future in the global economy.

The Petersen family owned the company for sixty-one years before selling it in 1985. In the following years Vise-Grip passed through more owners, but through it all the DeWitt plant remained central, producing the famous wrench, what the company called "the world's most versatile hand tool." In 2002 the company was bought by the Newell Corporation, a multinational corporation known for its rigorous cost cutting. Then everything changed.

Randy Badman remembers the time well. Badman was typical of so many in the plant: his father, mother, uncle, aunt, and grandfather had all worked there. He'd been there thirty-three years the day Newell arrived.

He had started as a tool and die maker, manually cutting the dies that were used to shape the components that were stamped out of molten steel by the plant's big presses. The plant did it all. "The raw steel came in one end, and the Vise-Grip went out the other," Badman said. In between, workers made virtually everything else: they forged the steel components, cut the teeth in the pliers, even made the screws, springs, and rivets that made the locking pliers unique.

In the 1980s, the plant had begun converting to computerized numerical control (CNC) machines to do the work long done by hand. When the first one arrived, the company sent Badman to

Omaha for training in how to program and operate the equipment that was revolutionizing factory floors across America. As more CNC machines arrived at the plant, Badman's responsibilities grew. Eventually he headed the entire thirty-nine-man round-the-clock department of tool and die makers. The new machines were reducing manual labor, but even with the new efficiencies employment grew, rising to more than six hundred.

After Newell bought the plant, the spirit that had powered decades of growth and job creation vanished. "Everyone had a very uneasy feeling when it was sold," Badman recalled. "You never know once a big corporation gets a hold of something."

Badman said it wasn't long before the new corporate owners began insisting on cuts—they told him to cut 5 percent in his budget. From then on, all he heard was, "You've got to cut, you've got to cut, you've got to cut." So, Badman said, "we gave them that, and then they wanted more. Once that started, we knew it was not going to be good."

Workers at the non-union plant took a series of voluntary pay cuts, and Badman said they took a hard look at all internal processes to see what could be streamlined. "We did all the things you can do," Badman said. Some changes made the plant more efficient, "but that can only go so far," Badman said. "When you get a little too far, then you have to stop and say, 'Okay, we've cut it to here. This is good. We're making good profits. Now let's run with it. Let's sell more because we're more efficient.'"

Early one morning in 2005, Badman was working at his desk when he saw his boss pass by on his way to human resources. Soon Badman was summoned to the same office. Seated behind a desk was a woman from Newell he did not know, and in front of her was a pile of papers. She told him to sign them. The company was "realigning," she said, and he was being dismissed. He was escorted through the plant and out the door of the factory where he'd worked for thirty-six years and told to contact HR for an appointment to come in and clean out his desk. That same day twelve other midlevel managers and supervisors, including Badman's boss, were fired. As bad as things had been, Badman was stunned. "You don't think that they're going to take out everybody who knew what was going on and who was running the place," he said.

Three years later, in 2008, Newell dismissed the remaining three hundred workers, closed the plant, and announced that Vise-Grip production would be shifted to China. In an instant, the low-slung sprawling factory that had been the lifeblood of DeWitt for eighty-four years fell silent.

"What you miss now is the hum—the hum of the factory," Badman recalled. "You could have your windows open on a summer evening and you'd hear the presses going up and down. And now there's silence. Nothing."

Looking back, Badman believes that Newell had no intention of keeping the plant going and that all its efforts were aimed at strangling it. Why else would they jettison the entire supervisory crew in one day and throw the place into turmoil unless they were planning to shut it down anyway?

"I think they wanted to squeeze us until they couldn't," he said. "Then they went overseas."

Badman's assessment was right on the money. If there were a Fortune 500 for wholesale terminations, Newell would rank near the top of the list. Two decades earlier, in 1987, Newell had purchased the Anchor Hocking Glass Corporation, one of the country's oldest glass container manufacturers. Within four months of the acquisition, a team of Newell executives swooped down on an Anchor Hocking plant in Clarksburg, West Virginia, where workers produced novelty glasses like the Star Wars and Camp Snoopy collections handed out by McDonald's during promotional campaigns. As Robert Trent, a personnel supervisor, told us in 1991 about a visit from the corporate owner in the fall of 1987:

> We were really excited about some Newell people coming down and looking at our facility, because we thought we were doing very well. They came in about ten in the morning. We saw them come in. They went to the plant manager's office . . . and told him they were closing this facility November 1, 1987. And that was it. They were out of here by ten-thirty.

With certain exceptions, the corporate takeover targets were profitable. They just were not as profitable as corporate raiders and Wall Street wanted. And they certainly were not profitable enough to pay bloated salaries to layers of executives.

In October 2011—three years after Newell closed the Vise-Grip plant—the hurt and the sense of loss in DeWitt were still palpable. Townspeople spoke longingly of the plant, of the positive influence it had on the town and their lives, and of the loss they continued to feel. DeWitt had lost its only grocery store. The longtime weekly newspaper had folded. Other businesses were pinched. A ready source of work for the town's young people—either as summer jobs or as careers for those who elected not to pursue higher education—was gone.

Former plant workers have tried to move on. Some went back to school for training to become home health aides or office workers. Some took jobs in other towns. Others retired early. Randy Badman has had three jobs in manufacturing since Vise-Grip and lost two of them to outsourcing. By late 2011, he was working as a foreman at a Nebraska foundry ninety miles from his home in DeWitt, where he and his wife Marge still live and where Randy serves as the town's mayor. He drives 180 miles round-trip four days a week to his new job. It's a grind, but he likes the work and the job provides health insurance for himself and his wife.

In most cases, former Vise-Grip workers who have been able to find work are earning less, and they've learned to live on less. They've tried to put the past behind them, but it comes rushing back when they come upon tool displays at a Home Depot or Lowe's and see the familiar yellow-and-blue packaging touting Vise-Grips as: "The Original. Since 1924."

Of course they aren't the original. The locking pliers are now made in a factory in the heavily industrialized city of Shenzhen, north of Hong Kong. Although they're produced under tight security in a limited-access industrial park, a former worker from DeWitt obtained an inside view of the Chinese operation after Newell hired him to try to straighten out production problems there.

A twenty-year veteran of DeWitt, Bruce McDougall arrived in China not long after the Nebraska plant closed to find the new Shenzhen operation in chaos. Components were arriving from multiple suppliers and were hard to track. There was no quality control on the production line. Newly manufactured tools broke or wouldn't work, he said. From the outside, the factory didn't look much different from plants in the States, but inside was another story. To McDougall, the place was like a time capsule, a throwback to earlier times when Vise-Grip's DeWitt plant relied on manual labor to make the tools.

"It looked more like Vise-Grip in 1950, when everything was made by hand," McDougall said, rather than like the highly automated plant that Newell had shut down in 2008 to be more "competitive." He said Newell kept throwing more and more bodies into the mix to increase production. But even with five times the workforce of DeWitt, McDougall said, production still faltered. "We were turning out fifty thousand tools a day at the end in DeWitt," he said. "Their best day in China was fifteen thousand with five times the number of people."

There were other contrasts too. In DeWitt, many Vise-Grip employees lived in neat, well-kept houses on quiet lanes not far from the plant, but in China Newell's workers were packed into dormitory-like quarters adjacent to the factory. Living conditions mirrored the chaos of the plant floor. As many as twelve workers were stuffed into cramped rooms for sleeping. "The night shift guy would go in and work twelve hours," McDougall said. "Then he'd go back to the dorm and wake up the day shift guy, who'd go in for twelve hours." McDougall spent three months in China and couldn't wait to leave. "The place was off the wall," he said. Even with the cheap labor, McDougall said it was costing Newell more to make the Vise-Grip in China when he was there than it had cost in DeWitt.

This was the height of economic insanity. A once-pathbreaking American industrial innovator, whose manufacturing processes had been successfully modernized by a company that was the anchor employer for an entire community, was sold not because greater economic efficiencies could be achieved elsewhere, let alone because quality or distribution could be improved. It was picked off by a rapacious corporation and dumped haphazardly thousands of miles away. A case of a short-term gain for a corporation, but at the expense of a sustainable economic future for a community.

The loss of the Vise-Grip plant was a betrayal of the people of DeWitt. The village clerk, Linda Schuerman, whose husband worked at the plant for decades, is deeply upset over Washington's indifference to working people and the impact it is having on communities such as DeWitt:

> I'm not a political person, but something's wrong with Washington, D.C. They are to blame. They should have kept the companies here. We are nosing our way into all these countries that don't want us and can't stand us when we should be helping our own people. All the people out here want to do is make a living and support their families.

Coming into DeWitt, visitors pass the massive, four-columned brick entry sign on Highway 103 that has welcomed visitors to the town for years: HOME OF THE VISE-GRIP TOOL. The town's website also pays tribute to the enterprise that brought prosperity and economic well-being to more than three generations, but it has had to adjust to the times. On the website, DeWitt is no longer the "home" of the Vise-Grip Tool, but its "birthplace." Like so many chapters in the story of American manufacturing, this one is now history.

THE BIRTH OF APPLE

Defenders of free trade and the ruthless corporate behavior that often accompanies it contend that the fate of companies such as Vise-Grip, while sad for those who lose their jobs, is merely part of a natural process of the American economy renewing itself.

The nation, they say, is constantly being reinvented as old industries and companies give way to new ones. Along the way, old jobs are eliminated or offshored. It's easy to assume that perhaps older companies such as Vise-Grip did not keep up with the times (though it did) or that its invention was no longer relevant (the Vise-Grip remains a hugely popular tool). But the story must be different for twenty-first-century innovators. Surely current innovations are valued more highly and treated more carefully so that their benefits can be shared by the communities that supported their creation? If only that were true. Look no further than the story of an iconic American company, Apple Computer.

The story has been told many times of how Steve Jobs and Steve Wozniak, tinkering with electronic components in the Jobses' family garage, built the first Apple computer in 1976 and launched the personal computer industry.

Like William Petersen of Vise-Grip a half-century earlier, Jobs and Wozniak had an idea, and their curiosity and ingenuity enabled them to create a new product from it. And like Vise-Grip, Apple was soon manufacturing its products for sale, first from a building south of San Francisco and then in an assembly plant in Fremont, California, on the other side of the Bay. Soon additional plants in Elk Grove, California, near Sacramento, and Fountain, Colorado, near Colorado Springs, would be turning out Apple computers. For the two new plants, the future looked especially bright.

Apple's Elk Grove plant, opened in 1992, became the centerpiece of Sacramento's campaign to attract high-tech companies.

Other computer makers soon followed. By the mid-1990s, the Sacramento area was considered the computer manufacturing capital of the United States. Apple's Elk Grove plant, which manufactured circuit boards and desktop computers, operated seven days a week and employed 1,500 persons.

About the same time, the Apple plant in Fountain went into production and soon became the company's largest manufacturing facility, turning out 1 million PowerBook and desktop computers a year. It was a state-of-the-art facility that helped the Colorado Springs area attract other high-tech companies. The emergence of this new industry was a relief to the area, which had long been dependent on the ups and downs of defense contracts from Washington.

Apple seemed to be following the classic path of industrial development that Vise-Grip and scores of other domestic manufacturers had taken for years. A creative entrepreneur invents a product, builds plants to make it, and markets it to consumers, all the while employing ever more people to build the product. This is win-win innovation.

But Apple changed the rules, and the story diverged from the pattern that U.S. manufacturers had followed for decades. Rather than continue to open new plants in other U.S. cities and expand existing operations, the company, following the examples of other computer and electronics makers, moved production offshore, largely to China. Just twelve years after it opened, the Elk Grove plant was closed, "cutting out the core of what used to be one of the brightest stars in the region's high-tech constellation," as the

Sacramento Bee put it. Apple sold the Fountain plant to an electronics firm in 1996. The new owners continued to manufacture Apple computers under contract for three years until
production there also moved abroad. Today the 250,000-
square-foot building sits vacant, a painful reminder of what was
once a thriving tech industry.

As recently as 2000, Colorado Springs was riding a high-tech
job boom. But since then, with the closure of the former Apple
plant and other facilities, the area has lost more than 40 percent of
its manufacturing and information technology jobs. More than
15,000 jobs—paying from $55,000 to $80,000 plus benefits—
simply vanished, according to local economic development officials, sucking an estimated $500 million out of the local economy.
In their place, jobs in call centers for insurance, finance, and cell
phones were created—jobs that paid about half of what the IT
jobs paid, according to local officials.

Bill Stamp was one of Apple's first employees at Fountain. He
was twenty-six years old when he joined the company in 1984 at
its Fremont assembly plant, recording and keeping track of the
myriad parts that went into each personal computer, from hard
drives to screws. When the company offered him an opportunity
to get in on the ground floor at its new assembly plant in
Colorado, he jumped at the chance. His wife-to-be, Christy, also
an Apple employee, landed a job at Fountain as well, and later
he moved up to a supervisory position in shipping. Gregarious
and down to earth, Stamp is the first to tell you he was never a

computer geek. He was a "materials guy" whose job was to feed the production line: "My job was to get it to the line and make sure it was a quality product ready for the line to use."

Apple instilled in him and his coworkers a quality control ethic that made them want to turn out the best possible product. "There was such a camaraderie," he said. "When we got off work, all we could talk about was Apple, Apple, Apple. We've got to do this or that. And we had the freedom, a process, to bring that up, and these things would then often come about. It was phenomenal, one big family." It was an exciting time. Stamp said the folks in the factory thought of themselves as responsible for helping to build the company. They were appreciated and well compensated, and they basked in the glow of working for Apple.

Stamp said that he and Christy moved into a comfortable bilevel house set on five acres near the Black Forest, an area of abundant ponderosa pines and natural beauty north of Colorado Springs. "We were living large," he said. "We thought it would go on forever."

But when earnings fell in 1996 and the moneymen on Wall Street decided Apple was not living up to their expectations, the company was forced to unload assets to raise cash. The Fountain plant was sold, just four years after it had opened. Fountain was profitable and well run, but Wall Street's relentless focus on short-term earnings demanded results. An Alabama-based electronics vendor and outsourcing specialist, SCI Systems Inc., bought Fountain for $75 million with an agreement to continue manufacturing Apple computers on-site for three years.

The plant's ownership wasn't the only thing that changed. Stamp recalled that the new managers were "arrogant as hell," dismissive of Apple veterans, and uninterested in feedback from employees. "What a culture shock that was," he said. After having worked in a collaborative environment that encouraged ideas from the ground up, the essence of a continuously innovative culture, all he ever heard from the Alabama imports were relentless orders to "git 'er done." When the contract to make Macs expired in 1998, Apple didn't renew, and the manufacturing shifted offshore.

Discouraged about Fountain's future, Stamp left in 2001. He tried his hand in real estate in Colorado and held a series of supervisory jobs at less pay in distribution and warehousing, first in Colorado and then in California. In 2008, when his job was shipped to Singapore, he hit a stone wall. Always before, he had been able at least to secure an interview that often led to a job— if only for a while. Now he would send out résumés listing his lengthy experience and wasn't even getting a call.

As the months ticked by, Stamp and his wife drew down their savings and tapped into retirement accounts to fund the fruitless quest for work and to try to hold on to their home. As so often happens, in the end they lost the home. For family reasons, they moved back to California in 2003 and settled in Milpitas, near San Jose, where they rented a two-bedroom apartment. In the summer of 2011—at the age of fifty-three, after he'd been out of work for three years—Stamp found a temporary job working as an inventory control analyst for a company in the Bay Area. It was a step down from supervising, and the job did not come with benefits, but at least he was working again.

Stamp remembers reading an article years ago, when he was still with Apple, predicting that the average worker in the future would undergo four different career changes and hold as many as ten different jobs. And he had thought: *Not me. I'm staying right here.* Little did he know that would never be an option.

That's because Congress, which writes the rules of employment, and Wall Street, which decides what rules it will permit, had other plans. The jobs that provided a good living for Stamp and thousands of other production workers in Fountain and Elk Grove are now in China. Almost every Apple product—Macs, iPods, iPhones, iPads—is made in China. Unlike in the past when companies manufactured in the United States for decades, Apple shipped its jobs offshore in less than a generation. So much for the benefits of American innovation to America.

Apple's move to China came about quietly and was little noticed at the time because of the way the company went about creating its offshore presence. Rather than build plants that proudly displayed the Apple name, as it did in California and Colorado, the company turned to firms that partnered with the Chinese to establish Apple plants in mainland China that bore the name of their Chinese contractor even though inside they were making

Apple products. This convenient buffering arrangement insulated Apple from oversight of its offshore workplaces.

Apple production workers in Fountain and Elk Grove bought homes, sent their kids to school, shopped locally, saved for their retirement, and, briefly, lived the American dream. That dream, or anything like it, has not been extended to their Chinese replacements.

In 2011, in a story for the Investigative Reporting Workshop, we told of how Apple's good-paying manufacturing jobs in the United States had been shifted overseas "to laborers in sweatshops in China." We contrasted the middle-class lifestyle and working conditions that Bill Stamp and other Apple production workers had enjoyed in the States with the grueling working and living conditions of workers making Apple products in China.

Prior to our story, reports had periodically surfaced in China about the exploitive and demeaning conditions that suppliers had imposed on these workers at various compounds where Apple products were made. Some of this reporting work was by a courageous Hong Kong–based human rights group called Students and Scholars Against Corporate Misbehavior (SACOM). Then, early in 2012, about two months after our investigation was published, the story went viral when the *New York Times* published lengthy accounts about worker abuse and harsh conditions.

The heart of Apple's production in China is near Shenzhen, a throbbing megalopolis of 10 million, less than an hour north of Hong Kong. Just outside the city is a massive, fortresslike compound surrounded by walls and protected by tight security where guards stop each vehicle at the entrance and check the identities of occupants by using fingerprint-recognition scanners.

Within the walled city are numerous factories, dormitories, support businesses, and an on-site television network, all humming around the clock. This is the Longhua Science and Technology Park, one of the densest concentrations of high-tech manufacturing in the world. Owned by Taiwan-based Foxconn Technology Group, the largest manufacturer of electronics and computer components in the world, Longhua is home to as many as 300,000 workers.

The workers labor in enormous factories, row after row of them bent over workstations that seem to stretch endlessly into the distance. They assemble iPods, iPhones, iPads, and products for other electronics makers. Occasionally, photos surface showing workers, mostly young women, wearing spiffy white coats and caps, going about their work in what appear to be pleasant, well-lit surroundings, just as workers once did at Elk Grove and Fountain.

But that's the only similarity with Apple's former plants in the United States.

iSLAVES

Workers at Longhua and other Foxconn plants in China usually work from ten to twelve hours a day, sometimes for seven days straight without overtime pay. They're not allowed to speak to each other on the job or to leave their workstations—not even to go to the bathroom—without permission from guards. Some of them perform repetitive tasks for up to ten hours at a time without a break. Supervisors berate workers with foul language and warn that if they fall behind on production they will be replaced. Some have reportedly been beaten for mistakes they allegedly made on the assembly line. For this, they earn little more than a dollar an hour at most.

SACOM, the Hong Kong human rights group, which has documented these practices in numerous reports, described working conditions at one Foxconn plant making iPhones: "Workers frequently endure excessive and forced overtime in order to gain a higher wage. If they cannot reach the production target, they have to skip dinner or work on unpaid overtime shifts." SACOM calls Foxconn's Apple workers "iSlaves."

Most young workers live on-site in cramped high-rise dormitories near the factories, where as many as a dozen workers squeeze into small rooms with three tiers of bunk beds. Most of them are peasants in their late teens or early twenties who have been lured to the city in hopes of earning money for themselves and their families back home, only to find themselves yoked to brutal production schedules that can become unbearable.

Upwards of two dozen workers at Apple plants in China have become so desperate that they have taken their own lives, often by jumping to their death from their dormitories. The deaths were so common for a time that Chinese bloggers began referring to the Shenzhen plant as the "Foxconn Suicide Express." In its investigation of conditions at Longhua and other plants making Apple products, SACOM concluded that many of those who committed suicide were exhausted, overworked, verbally and physically abused by supervisors, or publicly humiliated when they failed to meet their production quotas. SACOM reports tell the story of some of these young victims:

- Hou, a nineteen-year-old woman from Hunan province, hanged herself in the toilet of her dorm room on June 18, 2007, shortly after she had assured her parents that she would soon be coming home.
- Sun, a twenty-five-year-old college graduate from Yunnan province, jumped to his death from his twelfth-floor room on July 16, 2009, after he was allegedly blamed for losing a prototype for a new iPhone. According to SACOM, Sun was detained by security officers, placed in "solitary confinement," subjected to "psychological pressures," and allegedly beaten. In a final chat with friends shortly before he killed himself, he described the relief he felt in planning to take his own life: "Thinking that I won't be bullied tomorrow, won't have to be the scapegoat, I feel much better."
- After Feng, a twenty-three-year-old college graduate, jumped to his death from his fourteenth-floor room on

January 16, 2009, police found a suicide note: "Too much work pressure; unstable emotions."

- Ma, a nineteen-year-old native of Henan province, was found dead near a stairway of his dormitory on January 23, 2010. An autopsy concluded that he had fallen to his death. His sisters later insisted that their brother died from a beating he had suffered after he accidentally damaged equipment at work.

After a rash of suicides at the Foxconn plant in early 2010, Foxconn took action: it strung nets around the dorms to catch any workers who might try to kill themselves by jumping. It also sealed balcony doors and barred access to roofs. Workers were reportedly urged to sign a statement promising not to kill themselves and to "treasure their lives." Apple said later in a public report on "supplier responsibility" issued to shareholders that it was "disturbed and deeply saddened to learn that factory workers were taking their own lives" and pledged to take steps "to help prevent further tragedies." The company launched a search "for the most knowledgeable suicide prevention specialists" and commissioned a study so as to better "support workers' mental health in the future." Apple also commended its contractor Foxconn for taking "quick action," including "attaching large nets to the factory buildings to prevent impulsive suicides."

Once the nets were installed, the number of suicides dropped, but working conditions at Longhua and other Foxconn plants have changed little, if at all, according to SACOM. Although Apple pledged to work with Foxconn to improve conditions, in SACOM's view the company failed to follow through and insist on reforms, and so many of the conditions that prompted the suicides still exist. Similar conditions apparently prevail at other Foxconn plants that make products for other American manufacturers. About three hundred workers who assemble Microsoft XBoxes in central China threatened mass suicide from the roof of their factory in early 2012 over wage and working conditions, but were talked down by the town's mayor.

Following a new wave of revelations and criticism in the press in 2012 about working conditions in the factories of its Chinese suppliers, Apple CEO Tim Cook traveled to China to inspect plants where Apple products are made. An internal audit released afterward confirmed many of the charges of harsh working conditions where iPhones and iPads are made. Foxconn pledged to raise wages and improve conditions. Only time will tell if anything will change; in the past, similar pledges have been made to make life better for the workers.

After the suicides at Longhua, Foxconn and Apple stepped up plans to move more iPhone and iPad production inland to cities in central and western China, where there is even less oversight of living and working conditions. One major center for iPad production is now Chengdu in southwest China, nearly one thousand miles from Hong Kong. In its first year of production, an explosion, apparently caused when aluminum dust was ignited, rocked the plant, killing four workers and injuring eighteen others. SACOM investigators interviewed workers at Chengdu and found that many of the same conditions afflicting Apple workers at the plants on China's east coast were present at Chengdu: workers labored for hours at a time applying chemicals, sealants, and parts to iPads, assembling objects they knew they would never have the money to buy.

One young worker lamented that he couldn't even dream of owning an iPad because it would "cost two months' salary"—a far cry from the working conditions of the young Apple in its U.S. factories. Bill Stamp remembers a day early in his career when Apple, having asked workers to come in on a Saturday, gave everyone a new Macintosh as a bonus for a job well done. Everyone felt rewarded, properly included in the success of the ever-innovative Apple. But would innovators of the future allow themselves to dream of innovation if they thought it would inexorably lead to slavelike working conditions and suicides? Surely that isn't the end of the story of American innovation of the future?

To Stamp, it's amazing to realize how quickly it all changed—how the door to so much opportunity and a secure future suddenly slammed shut when Apple began to subcontract the making of its basic products and then shipped all the work to other countries.

Stamp sees his own future clearly. Like tens of millions of other Americans, he realizes that he will never be able to retire:

"I figure I'll drop over dead somewhere because I'll still be working," he says. If, that is, he can find work.

As for Apple, moving jobs abroad couldn't have worked out better. The corporation sometimes has more cash in its bank accounts than the U.S. Treasury. In January 2012, the company became the most valuable corporation on the planet—its stock was worth $422 billion, a sum that exceeded even the worth of Exxon Mobil Corporation, the world's largest international oil and gas company. For the Apple executives who sent the company's jobs offshore, the results have been especially rewarding. Tim Cook, who took over as Apple's CEO when Steve Jobs resigned shortly before his death, was handed a fat new compensation package in 2011 valued at nearly $380 million. That roughly equaled the pay of more than five thousand factory workers in America who still had jobs.

CHAPTER 4

PHANTOM JOBS

On his last day on the job, Kevin Flanagan, after clearing out a few personal effects and putting them in boxes in the back of his Ford Ranger, left the building where he'd worked for seven years. He settled into the front seat of his pickup truck on the lower level of the company garage, placed a twelve-gauge Remington shotgun to his head, and pulled the trigger.

He was forty-one years old. He was a computer programmer. He'd been a programmer his entire working life.

Until, that is, his job was shipped overseas. The business of moving traditional U.S. jobs abroad—called "outsourcing"—has been one of this country's few growth industries. It's the ultimate short-sighted business promoted by the country's elite because it means lower wages and fatter profits. As for the American workers eliminated along the way, they are just collateral damage.

Kevin was a casualty of the new American economy. Only a few years before, programmers like him were seen as some of the brightest lights of a modern American workforce as technology became the backbone of so many corporate operations.

Kevin was college-educated and hardworking by all accounts. He had compiled an impressive résumé with his last employer, Bank of America in Concord, California, and at previous jobs in the Bay Area and Los Angeles. His peers gave him high marks: One called him a "programming god." Another noted that "every time I got stuck on a program, he'd unstuck it in, like, ten seconds."

He was analytical by nature and loved to solve problems, but in the end he had no answer for the problem that had been dealt his profession.

His employer, Bank of America, did what so many companies now do to their employees. After years of dedicated service, one day they're told they're being replaced. Not because they haven't worked hard enough. Not because they aren't dedicated to their jobs. Not because they're not educated or qualified. They're being replaced because the company, thanks to federal policies, can hire someone else a lot cheaper.

Kevin's replacement was a programmer from India who had gained admission to the United States under a U.S. government program pushed through Congress by big business. Corporate lobbyists claimed the program was needed to ease a shortage of domestic programmers and computer specialists. In fact, it was a way for corporations to cut salaries.

Kevin was ordered to train his replacement or lose his modest severance package. It ripped him apart. Playing by all the rules had gotten him a pink slip.

It was a bitterly sad end for a talented professional. Kevin grew up in the Long Beach, California, area, the son of middle-class parents. His father worked for the famed aircraft maker Douglas Aircraft. His mother was a high school music teacher. In school, Kevin was inquisitive and loved to ask questions—he needed to know the "why" of everything, his father, Tom Flanagan, recalled fondly. Kevin was also captain of the high school debate team, which never lost a match.

He studied computer science and philosophy at California State University in Long Beach. After graduation, he worked as a programmer for McDonnell Douglas, and when that company began to falter before being acquired by Boeing, he moved to the San Francisco area and worked as a programmer at two companies before joining Bank of America in 1996. He was part of a small unit at the bank's Concord Technology Center, a four-building complex on San Francisco's East Bay where programmers wrote code on a myriad of money transfer transactions.

There Kevin felt he had found a home. His father said that his son liked his job and his colleagues and did well at the bank. He was even offered a promotion to move to one of the bank's East Coast facilities, but he declined.

"Kev wanted to stay where he was," said Tom Flanagan. "He was content with his small group of programmers, with the job, and with the little house he bought in Pleasant Hill."

But then, in his father's words, "the hammer began to strike." The bank began shipping some work offshore and importing programmers from India as guest workers, courtesy of the U.S. government. Bank of America had cut a deal in 2002 with an offshore provider based in India to oversee part of this work transfer.

The outsourcing was bad enough. Flanagan found himself called upon to clean up some of the mistakes that came in from overseas. Week after week Kevin saw his little group of programmers whittled down. As more foreign guest workers arrived, one after another of his longtime programming colleagues was let go. Finally his unit was down to one—him. Even though "he knew it was only a matter of time," his father said, Kevin nevertheless was "totally disgusted" by the order to train his replacement. That might have "tipped him over the edge," his father said, though no one saw it at the time.

On what he knew would be his last day of work, April 17, 2003, Kevin met with a bank official from Chicago who had been sent in to do the firing. The official later told police that he had met with Flanagan the morning of the day he committed suicide, explained his severance package, and asked him to turn in any company property in his possession. The official told police that Kevin, ever professional, was in "good spirits and had been taking it well."

For the Flanagan family, the wounds are still fresh. They lost a son and brother, and America lost a good mind, in Tom Flanagan's words. They knew Kevin was upset. They knew he felt betrayed by the company that he'd given so much to for years. But they had no idea that he was "so desperately in need of help."

Kevin Flanagan didn't lose his job by accident. Outsourcing is not a freak occurrence of nature like an earthquake or hurricane, although we often use metaphors like that to describe what it feels like for those on the wrong end of it. Kevin Flanagan lost out because the economic policies that those in power have imposed on America guarantee that jobs like his will be eliminated. Of course, they never told Kevin that when he went off to college to study computer science.

Any product or service in America can be imported or outsourced with little or no duty, regardless of where or how it is made. The product may be produced cheaply under dangerous conditions, in a nation with no labor standards or environmental regulations. But to the folks who run the country, that's okay. *Sorry,* they say, *but American workers will have to pay the price. That's just the way it's going to be. That's the market at work.*

This is *not* the market at work—this is the market they created that works for them. The ruling class sold the idea of opening the country to an unrestricted flow of imports on the basis that American society as a whole would benefit: we would buy from other countries, and they would buy from us. But from the start there has never been a balance. No safeguards were ever put in place to prevent other nations from taking advantage of our open-door policy to sell us goods produced under conditions that made their cost artificially low. One of the central manufacturing costs is the price of labor. Inevitably, the consequence of inviting foreign firms into the American market is that labor costs fall to the level of the lowest suppliers.

Global free trade is an invitation to cut the cost of labor at home or, even more profitably, shift jobs abroad. Like so many other chapters in the nation's trade history, the shipment of work offshore began imperceptibly as a way for companies to trim costs, and was seemingly so inconsequential in the beginning that it appeared to pose no threat to U.S. workers.

America essentially invented outsourcing, but few outside the corporate world realized how rapidly it, along with other trade policies, would devastate employment across the middle class as imports quickly overwhelmed exports and workers in industry after industry were sacrificed on the altar of unrestricted free trade.

For the ruling class, this was just fine. Everything was proceeding along the lines of their free market theories. They wanted no restrictions on trade policy, and Congress obliged. They wanted complete freedom to close plants in the United States, set up plants offshore, and outsource work to anywhere in the world without any tax penalty, and Congress obliged. They wanted to stonewall the wage demands of workers back home by hinting that their jobs might be ticketed for the next offshore shuttle if they asked for too much, and Congress went along. With this kind of oversight, was any job safe?

Kevin Flanagan certainly thought his field was safe when he entered it in the 1980s. Computer programming looked like one of the surefire careers for the future. Everyone said so. The advent of large mainframe computers in the 1960s had kicked off the first big increase in jobs, and the demand for programmers rose even more in the late 1970s with the introduction of personal computers and the extension of data processing into more and more businesses. Everyone thought that even bigger growth in programming jobs lay ahead.

In its 1990–1991 *Occupational Outlook Handbook,* a biennial publication that forecasts the future of occupations in the United States, the U.S. Department of Labor was especially bullish: "The need for programmers will increase as businesses, government, schools and scientific organizations seek new applications for computers and improvements to the software already in use [and] further automation . . . will drive the growth of programmer employment." The report predicted that the greatest demand would be for programmers with four years of college, who would earn above-average salaries.

When the Department of Labor made these projections in 1990, there were 565,000 computer programmers in the United States, but with computer usage expanding, the department predicted, "employment of programmers is expected to grow much faster than the average for all occupations through the year 2005."

It didn't. Employment fluctuated in the years following the report, then settled into a slow downward slide after 2000. By

2002, the number of computer programmers in the United States had slipped to 499,000. That was down 12 percent from 1990—not up. Nonetheless, the Labor Department was still optimistic that the field would create jobs—if not at the robust rate the agency had predicted, then at least at the same rate as the economy as a whole.

Wrong again. By 2006, even that illusion couldn't be maintained. When the number of jobs fell to 435,000—130,000 fewer than in 1990—the Labor Department finally acknowledged that jobs in computer programming were "expected to decline slowly." It was a telling confession of a huge miscalculation: computer programming and the kind of work it represented—skilled work that usually required a bachelor's or higher degree—had been assumed to be beyond the capabilities of competitors from abroad with their less vaunted educational systems and lack of English language skills. They couldn't take that away from Americans, could they? But they did.

The reason? While some in Congress are simply ignorant about trade matters, a lot of free trade legislation is passed because people with money want it and make sure the money gets to those who vote. In spite of strong evidence put forth at the time of NAFTA about what would happen to jobs—which ultimately turned out to be accurate—Congress ignored it. From 1990, when Labor made its rosy prediction that programming jobs would increase at a faster rate than other jobs over the next fifteen years, the U.S. workforce grew by 24 percent. If the number of programmers had increased at just the pace of the overall workforce—let alone at the optimistic rate that Labor had once projected—at least 700,000 programmers would have been employed by 2006. Instead, there were only 435,000. The job opportunities have continued to decline: in 2008, the last year for which figures are available, the number had dropped to 427,000. Even that number masks the magnitude of the domestic job losses. For among those 427,000 programmers were thousands of H-1B guest workers—foreign nationals brought in by U.S. companies, as allowed by immigration law, to do programming, usually at much lower pay and benefits. Like the guest worker who took Kevin Flanagan's job.

Washington attributes the unexpected U-turn on programming jobs to numerous factors, but the most telling cause was not even on its radar screen in 1990, even though it was already etched into the DNA of corporate America—offshoring. "Because they can transmit their programs digitally," the Labor Department belatedly admitted in 2006, "computer programmers can perform their job function from anywhere in the world, allowing companies to employ workers in countries that have lower prevailing wages."

In place of well-paid programming jobs in the U.S., the growth fields in the two decades after 1990 were for home health aides, retail clerks, customer service agents, truck drivers, security guards, and child care workers—low-paying jobs with few opportunities for advancement or better pay.

Domestic programmers, like millions of workers in other fields, are casualties of a Congress long indifferent to the plight of American workers. Rather than create a level economic playing field, lawmakers and presidents, both Democrat and Republican, have permitted foreign governments to set American job policies by eroding this country's basic industries. While free-traders in the United States have been busy honking their horns against any form of government intervention in the market, they have turned a blind eye to what has been going on in the globalized world they are so proud of having created. Many foreign governments ignore such theories and subsidize industries that they believe will help their people. In the 1980s, the government of India began supporting its nascent software industry in order to encourage companies to produce software for export. India's software exports totaled a mere $10 million in 1985; by 2010 they had reached an estimated $55 *billion.*

That dramatic increase came about because the Indian government in 1986 designated information technology as a high-priority industry with tremendous growth potential. The government then enacted incentives for attracting foreign investment and spurring industrial development to "enable the software industries to commence their operation with a minimum gestation period," as an Indian government report put it.

In 1991 the Indian government went a step further and created software technology "parks" throughout the country where the government provided space, electrical power, satellite hookups, streamlined procedures for export, and tax exemptions. In other words, the Indian government did what the U.S. government almost never does—it targeted a crucial industry for major government support. And it picked a winner: just ask unemployed U.S. computer programmers.

In what will spell even more trouble for America's remaining programmers, the Chinese are rapidly trying to catch up to India and are taking the competition to a new level. Like the Indian government, the Chinese government is providing incentives to foster a software development industry and has selected cities to pursue the software export strategy. In a sign of how aggressively they are marketing this industry, the Chinese have dispensed with the term "software parks." They are tactlessly but honestly calling the new centers what they truly are: outsourcing hubs. According to a study by Duke University's Offshoring Research Network, China has "mounted a vigorous challenge to India's software development outsourcing industry. More and more U.S. and European companies are outsourcing software and I.T. services directly to Chinese service providers."

The U.S. government is still very interested in creating programmer jobs—just not in this country. In 2010 the U.S. Agency for International Development (USAID) put up $10 million to help Sri Lanka develop an outsourcing industry. U.S. taxpayer dollars are aimed at training Sri Lankans in advanced IT skills like Enterprise Java, as well as in business process outsourcing and call center support. The goal is to create three thousand jobs.

According to *Information Week,* a similar program is being funded by USAID in Armenia to train Armenians. Perhaps even more countries are slated to get U.S. taxpayer money to develop their software industries. By then there may be no need to help U.S. programmers. There won't be any.

Service jobs in fields such as programming once were thought of as a key to America's future. As factory jobs were decimated by the imports encouraged by federal policies, service jobs were to take their place. America was in transition, we were told—the brawny factories with their bellowing forges and thunderous stamping machines were simply giving way to entirely new workplaces with sleek workstations housed in office towers.

Sure, it was sad about all those people losing their factory jobs to imports, but foreign competition would make our remaining plants more competitive, and the upheaval would be just a pit stop on the way to a bright postindustrial America. The future might seem bleak to anyone who worked in a factory that made cars or shoes, but the nation as a whole would adjust and move on to greater things. America always adapts, we were told. Isn't that what makes America great?

But there were fatal flaws in this theory. The first was that America's corporate leaders—executives and their boards—saw quickly that they could make enormous profits producing goods offshore rather than reinvesting at home. Labor was cheap abroad, and the developing countries would do anything to get the jobs. And as Apple discovered in China, none of these other countries were subject to the regulations that U.S. companies had to adhere to: fair labor standards, workplace safety rules, environmental standards—all rules that most Americans supported to make the nation a more livable place. As a bonus, thanks to corporate lobbying, whatever these U.S. companies made abroad under primitive conditions using slave labor they could bring back to the United States paying little or no import tax.

The other flaw in the theory, and the one that will be causing grief for working Americans for years to come, is that while China and India may be poor countries, each has millions of very bright, talented people eager to work at a fraction of what bright, talented people need in the United States to maintain a middle-class lifestyle here.

The first of the service jobs to be outsourced in great numbers were the back-office operations of banks, investment houses, insurance companies, and any business that processed huge amounts of paper, from credit card charges to procurement manifests to legal exhibits. Most of this work went to India, and as the industry grew, American corporations began sending more work there. Soon programmers in India were writing code and shipping it back to the United States. Other companies established call centers to field customer inquiries from the United States, and soon they too began to take on more complex tasks. Most large American health insurers now have call centers in India where workers answer questions following a highly detailed script on a computer screen. It is a multibillion-dollar-a-year industry that employs millions—in India. No one knows how many jobs this strategy has cost Americans, but who's counting? We still have those smart jobs, the creative ones—don't we?

Even the jobs requiring ingenuity and brain power are going too. The earlier phase of outsourcing was known as business process outsourcing (BPO). The latest is called knowledge process outsourcing (KPO). The corporate focus has expanded to the highly sophisticated operations that represent, in the words of one management consultant, the "very heart of the business . . . involving complex analytics." Where an earlier generation in India might have been reconciling credit card balances, today they perform statistical analyses, run growth projections, and do all the other things that number crunchers back home do—or once did.

The global consulting firm KPMG explained the appeal of KPO in a 2008 report: "Knowledge process outsourcing (KPO) enables clients to *unlock their top line growth by outsourcing their core work to locations that have a highly skilled and relatively cheap talent pool*" (our italics). This phrase should send a shudder down any economist's spine because it says out loud, albeit with a bit of jargon, the truth that cannot be spoken if you believe in a growing economy and shared prosperity: companies can get richer by moving the essence of what they do to cheaper countries. Why be located in the United States at all?

Advances in technology, along with rising education levels in India and other low-wage countries, have eased the reservations that many corporations once had about outsourcing and off-shoring, according to KPMG. In its view, KPO is unstoppable.

An ever-greater share of sophisticated analytics as well as creative jobs that were once done by middle-class Americans are being shipped offshore. Indian vendors create advertising copy, high-end photography, marketing brochures, graphic art, original illustration, and even music videos for the U.S. market—all at a fraction of what that work would cost in the States.

"Outsource your creative design services . . . and see your ideas taking form," says Outsource2india, a Bangalore-based firm. "Outsource2india offers a wide array of creative design services which include Graphic Design Services, Cover Design Services, Artwork Services, Illustration Services and Photography Services. Our professional graphic designers, creative illustrators and skilled photographers can meet all your design needs, be it a cover design for your music DVD, professional wildlife photographs, illustrated characters for your book, conversions of your rough sketches and much more.

"At Outsource2india, we provide high-quality and creative design services at a low cost. By outsourcing design services to India, you not only benefit from low costs but also benefit from our professional and creative design services."

Outsourcing is beloved by management consultants, and none more so than Accenture. The world's largest consulting firm, Accenture is a $25 billion a year global enterprise and a far cry from its days as a modest unit within the Arthur Andersen accounting empire in the United States.

Since branching out on its own, Accenture has reaped untold riches helping U.S. companies send work out of the country. Far and away the most successful outsourcer, the company is referred to on Wall Street as the "outsourcing giant." Accenture doesn't dispute the claim. The company says its "outsourcing services touch every industry and business process." Every year Accenture is voted the "top outsourcing service provider globally" by professionals in the industry, a distinction that a spokesman says the company earns by taking "outsourcing deeper" than others.

Deep into its own ranks, it turns out. Petitions are on file with the Labor Department by onetime Accenture employees in Atlanta, Georgia; Birmingham, Alabama; Chicago, Illinois; Dayton, Ohio; Morristown, New Jersey; Richfield, Minnesota; Wilmington, Delaware; and other cities. Their jobs as software developers, global management consultants, accountants, and financial agents were eliminated by Accenture in the United States and shipped to Argentina, Brazil, India, the Philippines, and other countries.

Whatever you say about Accenture, the company practices what it preaches.

THE EPICENTER OF IT

It was one of the best places to work in Tampa. The salaries were good. The benefits were excellent. Turnover was rare. And every year the company hosted a lavish holiday party. In a city with a large high-technology presence, PricewaterhouseCoopers (PwC) always ranked high in ratings compiled by the local press on the best places to work in the area. That's what made the events of July 29, 2010, so shocking.

The word had come down that day that everyone in information technology was to attend a company webcast that afternoon. Webcasts were broadcast every so often, and employees often skipped them. But this time the message was firm: everybody had to attend. Even members of the skeleton crew who manned the help line 24/7 when others were in staff meetings had to attend. *Shut down the phones. Be there.* One manager thought to herself, *This can't be good news.*

The webcast opened with a PwC official giving details about the company's financial picture, its revenue and profits. Then, a few minutes into his talk, he suddenly switched topics. The subject was the company's strategic plan. PwC had decided to outsource the work of its information technology division to India. It occurred so fast, and with so little warning, that it took people a few seconds to realize what had happened: they were all losing their jobs.

By year's end, about eight hundred employees would be gone. The cuts were staggered over months to give PwC's new IT contractor, Tata Consultancy Services of India, time to learn the jobs of the people PwC was firing. It was one of the largest mass dismissals ever in Tampa, but what was especially ominous were the kinds of positions eliminated.

PwC's huge Tampa operation was the "epicenter for nearly all the IT staff that supported the U.S. market," in the words of one former employee. Among their responsibilities was to build, manage, and maintain operating systems and the hardware supporting them for PwC partners and staff in the United States. To do so meant not only riding herd on temperamental computer networks but dealing with thousands of individual servers throughout the country. The men and women who held these sophisticated jobs were often college-educated, and were well versed in multiple software applications, database management, and the intricacies of managing a far-flung internal network that served thousands of PwC personnel. In other words, they had all the skills that supposedly count in the new American economy.

The jobs paid well, but they could be extremely stressful, especially when it came to keeping a galaxy of networks and servers all functioning in tandem. Anyone who has lost their Internet connection knows the frustration of trying to get back online. The problem is magnified at a commercial venture such as PwC, where millions of dollars can be at stake if connectivity is disrupted for an extended period. It was not uncommon for members of some of PwC's teams to work sixty to eighty hours a week to keep all the systems running. In one sector called platform services, one specialist worked every weekend for months without a break, according to Mark Ferneau, a former member of this team.

The Tampa office was part of PwC US, the American arm of the $29 billion global accounting and consulting behemoth based in the United Kingdom. The company, which is privately held with ownership in the hands of about eight thousand partners, discloses few financial details, but the Ames Research Group estimated the average gross earnings of partners at $872,640 in 2008—meaning, of course, that many earned in the millions. Although as a private company it wasn't answerable to Wall Street or stockholders, PwC had started to act like a publicly held company even before the mass layoffs.

Despite its reputation in Tampa as employee-friendly, in the years leading up to the layoffs the company had been engaging in belt-tightening moves that were out of character. Retiring employees weren't replaced. Other longtime employees were let go on a piecemeal basis for reasons that made no sense to their colleagues other than to cut costs. As one former IT employee later told the *St. Petersburg Times:* "It used to be a great place to work. They took care of their workers." But by the time of the layoffs in 2010, he said, it had become "a company of bean counters, and all they care about is saving a few pennies."

One of the divisions hit especially hard was the help desk headed by Irene Odell, who had worked at PwC for eleven years. A one-hundred-person operation, the desk was manned around the clock to field calls and requests from partners and other staff across the United States. The PwC help desk wasn't like the help desks that consumers contact when they want to question a bill or order a product. It was an integral part of the company's executive structure and business, always on call to resolve technical

computing problems, connectivity issues, password glitches—
any problem that had to be dealt with immediately.

A first-generation Greek American, Odell had graduated from
the University of South Florida with a degree in business administration in 1990. But she quickly found out that "it was not a
good time to be a brand-new graduate with a business degree,"
she said. When she couldn't find anything but minimum-wage
jobs, she realized that "this isn't what I want for the rest of my
life." So she went back to school to become a nurse. There she
became fascinated with computers and the rapidly emerging Internet. She started a website and became active with newsgroups
through Usenet, tried her hand at building websites, and became
proficient in using the new personal computer software that was
constantly arriving. By the time she earned her nursing degree in
1995, there was such a demand for people with computer experience that she went into IT, first at a small company in the
Tampa area, and then in 2000 at PricewaterhouseCoopers.

After losing her job, Odell wondered what she would do next.
She had the qualifications and résumé to land another job in IT,
though IT jobs were scarce in the Tampa Bay area. But the more
she thought about it the more she felt that there was no future for
IT in the United States. As she wondered whether to change careers, a meeting at PwC helped Odell make up her mind.

Like others who were on their way out the door, she attended
counseling sessions arranged by the company to help them with
their "transition." At one meeting she attended with about sixty

others, the employees were asked what they were thinking about doing next.

"Every single person was choosing a different field," she said. "Not one person said, 'I'm going to be looking for the kind of job I was doing.'"

One said she was going to nursing school. Another decided to open a cake decorating business.

"If I'd had any doubts about making a complete career change, that settled it for me," she said. "Because PwC had really smart people, and if all these really smart people are saying they want training for some other field, then collectively as a group we must be right."

She decided to return to nursing, the field where she'd earned her second degree before she went to work in IT. She had to go back to school to refresh her training, and she also had to obtain her nursing license. While in school, she took a nursing job at an acute-care facility, but cutbacks there created staff shortages and made working conditions extremely stressful.

Odell isn't sure that she will stay in nursing, but wherever she winds up, she knows she'll be earning much less than she earned at PricewaterhouseCoopers. Still, she feels fortunate. Her husband, a pharmacist, has a good job, so they'll be okay.

Others are not as fortunate. Alex Sanabria also worked in PwC's IT unit when he was fired in 2010. After he lost his job, Sanabria couldn't find work in Tampa. The recession there was still raging, and there was a glut of unemployed technology workers. First, he and his wife drew down their savings to try to keep their home, which they had bought at the top of the real estate market five years earlier. But they finally had to walk away and declare bankruptcy. For Sanabria, bankruptcy was "the most gut-wrenching, awful thing I've ever had to do." Eventually he and his wife moved to Colorado to live with her parents while he looked for work there. He finally found a job on the help desk of a consumer products company. He was working again, but at a much lower salary than at PwC.

Almost as bad as the economic blow was the emotional impact. PwC was Sanabria's first real job after college, and he says that he put his "heart and soul" into it, sometimes working sixty-five to seventy hours a week. He said he always got high marks and was moving up, taking on more responsibilities and earning raises and bonuses. Led to believe by his performance evaluations that the company valued his work, he had the feeling that "good things are coming around the corner."

What came around was a security escort out of the building. Like many people who lose their job, he began to doubt himself after he was fired. "You start wondering—and I don't think this way now—but you start thinking, *Maybe I wasn't a good employee. Maybe they had a reason to let me go.* I know that's the wrong way to think. I know I went in there and did the best job I could have possibly done every day I was there, but you start getting so demoralized."

Irene Odell says that she and many of her former coworkers will move on, but she does worry about what is happening to the middle class. With their expenses going up and their earnings going down, they have less and less income, and the gap between most Americans and those at the top keeps on growing. She wonders:

"When we get down the road and we end up where we're headed—which is an elite class and a low class—is the low class going to tolerate that for a long period of time? Isn't that what inspired the revolution?"

NEXT TO GO

One of the most overlooked—and most frightening—forecasts about the future of the middle class was released in December 2008. This was a study by researchers at the Labor Department that identified service jobs that might go offshore. Despite its scholarly tone, its conclusions are alarming.

It found that as many as 160 service occupations—one-quarter of the total service workforce, or 30 million jobs—could go offshore. Jobs in those 160 categories were growing at a faster rate than service jobs overall and, ominously for future middle-class incomes, they were among the higher-paying service jobs. The Bureau of Labor Statistics calculated the annual wage for these jobs at $61,473—significantly higher than the $41,610 in annual wages for all service occupations.

The list of vulnerable jobs and their average annual earnings is breathtaking: aerospace engineers ($92,700); aircraft mechanics ($49,670); anthropologists ($55,490); architectural drafters

($45,280); biochemists ($85,290); chemical engineers ($84,240); chemists ($68,520); epidemiologists ($63,600); fashion designers ($71,170); financial analysts ($81,700); graphic designers ($45,340); insurance underwriters ($60,120); market research analysts ($66,980); mathematicians ($90,930); microbiologists ($66,430); multimedia artists ($61,010); nuclear technicians ($65,850); pharmacists ($98,960); and tax preparers ($34,890).

The most revelatory aspect of the BLS report was how surprised by its conclusions its authors seemed to be. The agency that specializes in economic matters affecting working Americans has spent little time looking at what may be an Armageddon for service workers. But that's in keeping with the perennial optimism that economists generally peddle about the direction of the American economy when the subject involves free trade. Why give much ink, these optimists reason, to a problem that doesn't fit the prevailing theory that offshoring is good?

One of the few economists who did sound an alarm on offshoring, Alan S. Blinder of Princeton, was roundly criticized by his fellow economists when he predicted in 2007 that the offshoring of service jobs from rich countries to poor countries "may pose major problems for tens of millions of American workers over the coming decades."

While it's clear that free trade, as practiced by the United States, is driving down the income of millions of working Americans, the economically elite are sticking to their message that America is on the right track.

Harvard economist N. Gregory Mankiw, a former chairman of the Council of Economic Advisers under President George W. Bush, says that the migration of jobs from offshoring makes economic sense and is "the latest manifestation of the gains from trade that economists have talked about at least since the days of Adam Smith. . . . More things are tradable than were tradable in the past, and that's a good thing." For decades, Americans have been given misleading assurances like that. Many so-called experts have also made rosy predictions about the U.S. trade deficit. In a *Washington Post* article in 1992, Stephen Cooney, a senior policy director for international investment and finance for the National Association of Manufacturers, predicted that because of changes under way in the American economy, "with luck our trade deficit could disappear by 1995." No such luck. In 1992, when Cooney made his prediction, the deficit was $39 billion. Rather than disappearing by 1995, the deficit nearly tripled to $96 billion, and it has continued to escalate; by 2011 the trade deficit had reached $560 billion.

Gary Clyde Hufbauer, a former deputy assistant secretary at the Treasury Department, predicted in a research paper that was widely picked up by the media that NAFTA would "generate a $7 to $9 billion [trade] surplus that would ensure the net creation of 170,000 jobs in the U.S. economy the first year." Instead, NAFTA caused an immediate trade deficit with Mexico. By 2012, the cumulative total was $700 billion. More importantly, NAFTA wiped out hundreds of thousands of good-paying manufacturing jobs in the United States.

Hufbauer is still in the job-predicting business at a Washington think tank. One of his latest: "When American multinationals go overseas, on balance, they create more jobs here in the United States than they would have if they'd not gone overseas."

Right.

THE EDUCATION TRAP

If free trade isn't working out for millions of middle-class Americans, the elite have the answer. American workers need more education. If they upgrade their skills, they can compete in the global economy.

One of the promoters of this theory is Thomas Friedman, the *New York Times* columnist and author of the blockbuster bestseller *The World Is Flat*. Friedman maintains that our trade policies "must be accompanied by a focused domestic strategy aimed at upgrading the education of every American, so that he or she will be able to compete for the new jobs in a flat world." This is one of the most shopworn theories about what has caused our trade deficit and why we have lost so many jobs to offshoring and outsourcing. And it's wrong. The real cause is a failure of the trade policy in the first place.

In fact, what education has done is create a false sense of security. The theory that all you need is a sheepskin and jobs will seek you out is not rooted in reality. To begin with, not everyone benefits from a college education. Truth to tell, tens of millions of Americans don't benefit from higher education, but that doesn't mean their potential contributions to society are any less worthwhile. To suggest that their contributions are insignificant is arrogant and also ignores the basic rules of the labor market. Flooding a jobs sector with new applicants can have only one result: lower wages for everyone, which is exactly what is happening.

Today young Americans have more education than ever, but it's not doing them much good. The entry-level hourly earnings of college graduates today are lower than a decade ago: $21.77 in 2010 compared with $22.75 in 2000, according to the Economic Policy Institute (EPI). This decline had little to do with the 2008–2009 recession. EPI data show that earnings of recent grads fell all through this past decade. In fact, entry-level wages have barely risen in the last three decades. While a degree is better than no degree, there are "really no safe havens—even for college graduates," says Carl E. Van Horn, a professor of public policy at Rutgers University. "Everyone needs to calibrate, to readjust their expectations to meet the harsh realities that show little sign of letting up."

Even worse, more and more graduates leave college with suffocating debt loads that will make it impossible for many to achieve the lifestyles of their parents.

By the end of 2011, total outstanding student loan debt in the United States totaled more than $1 trillion—more than all credit card debt. The average college student graduates with a debt of about $24,000. Some owe $100,000 or more. Overall, student debt is growing by $100 billion a year. Those with a vested interest assure students they are not merely borrowing money, but investing in their futures. For some, it's true. For many, it isn't.

This trend creates a domino effect in the economy. It means that young people, the traditional first-time homebuyers, are unable to obtain a mortgage, hence priced out of the market. This further impacts the already dismal prospects of the homebuilding industry. The previous generation of homeowners, now ready to move up, can't because the pool of potential buyers for their homes has shrunk. Lastly, there can be no meaningful economic recovery until the housing sector rights itself. Since 2006, the country, under the guidance of Wall Street, Washington, and the super-rich elites, has run up $7 trillion in housing losses. As the Federal Reserve explains in its dry, understated way: "Declines on this scale are unprecedented since the Great Depression." Only the morbidly optimistic believe that any of this can be fixed within the foreseeable future.

Forty years ago, student loan debt was such a non-issue that it barely registered as a liability in America. The rising cost of college has been a major reason for the growth of student debt, but a parallel cause has been the economic collapse of the American middle class. In years past, many middle-class parents could save enough to pay for the education of their children. No more.

The amount of student debt was relatively unchanged throughout the 1970s, but in the 1980s—a period that coincided with growing problems of middle-income families—student debt began to spike. From 1999 to 2011, it recorded the sharpest rise yet, increasing 511 percent.

The result is that growing numbers of young American college graduates begin their working lives (if they're lucky enough to have a job) deep in debt and have no money to save, buy a home, or start a business—all the options of earlier generations.

More and more of them default on their loans. The U.S. Department of Education estimated defaults at nearly 9 percent in 2011, but other sources, including the *Chronicle of Higher Education,* say that the actual default rate is much higher, at least 20 percent. Whatever the number, default often makes the plight of borrowers much worse.

In 2005, bowing to the wishes of Wall Street and the financial industry, Congress passed a law that made it much harder for anyone to file for bankruptcy. The Bankruptcy Abuse Prevention and Consumer Protection Act came down especially hard on those struggling with their student loans by making it next to impossible for anyone with college loans to seek relief in bankruptcy court.

Student loans are the only form of debt for which bankruptcy isn't an option. Instead, borrowers have to undergo a costly process called "loan rehabilitation" run by companies holding the debt, a process that piles on more charges and plunges them even deeper in the hole. "This effectively obligates the borrower to a much larger debt than when the loan defaulted, often double, triple, or even more than the original loan amount," according to StudentLoanJustice.org, a grassroots group.

This means that many Americans who have college loans will never pay them off, says Nicholas Pardini, a Villanova University graduate student in finance who has followed and blogged on the issue. Instead, he says, they'll be relegated to a "lifetime of debt slavery."

Debt slavery at home or iSlavery abroad? With those consequences, can we really be proud of the trade policy we've been following for the last thirty years?

CHAPTER 5

THE
GREAT
TAX HEIST

M ost Americans agree that the rich should pay more taxes. Poll after poll indicates that a majority—including even a few billionaires such as Warren Buffet—would like to see higher taxes on the wealthy.

But it hasn't happened. And it isn't likely to happen. The ruling class won't let it happen.

In today's America a minority sets policy for the majority, the opposite of what democracy should be.

Two numbers starkly tell the story:

In 1955 the richest Americans—the four hundred households with the highest incomes—paid 51.2 percent of their income in federal taxes.

In 2007, on the eve of the global financial meltdown, the four hundred richest Americans paid 16.6 percent of their income in federal taxes.

The figures do not come from some liberal soak-the-rich think tank: they're from the Internal Revenue Service, part of the periodic number-crunching that the IRS performs on tax returns.

The victory of the ruling class has been more decisive in setting tax policy than in any other area, with trade running a close second. Three decades of tax cuts have lowered tax rates for corporations as well as the wealthy. Some of those savings have been reinvested in Washington so the victors could hold on to their gains and seek more. It's no coincidence that campaign contributions and lobbying expenditures have surged in the last generation, and they will continue to escalate.

After buying Congress, the super-rich secured a stamp of approval from the U.S. Supreme Court, which in 2010 gave its blessing to unlimited campaign contributions to a candidate by anyone with the money—individual or corporation. This means it will be harder and harder for the will of the people to override the money machine of the ruling class. A sign held by a protester at Occupy Wall Street in the fall of 2011 framed the issue: I DON'T MIND YOU BEING RICH. I MIND YOU *BUYING MY* GOVERNMENT!

The tax cuts for those at the top have greatly exacerbated inequality in America. Equally devastating is their effect on the deficit and what that will mean to the middle class for years to come. The tax cuts for the wealthy from 2001 to 2008 cost the

U.S. Treasury $700 billion in lost tax revenue. To cover the short-fall, Treasury printed more money and added $700 billion to the national debt. Paying interest on that debt will fall on many middle-class taxpayers for decades.

Having added to the national debt, the wealthy are now funding initiatives that decry the deficit and call for cuts in programs that provide safety nets for middle-class Americans such as Social Security and Medicare.

Meanwhile, during the period when the richest Americans received their enormous tax cuts, the taxes on the middle class actually went up. In 1960 the middle 20 percent of U.S. taxpayers paid 15.9 percent of their income in total federal taxes. By 2007, the same group of taxpayers was paying 16.1 percent, according to a report by the Wealth for Common Good, a Boston-based network of business leaders and wealthy individuals that advocates a more equitable tax system.

During World War II, most Americans—both corporations and individuals—contributed a fair share through an income tax that was progressive: those who could afford to pay more did so. The very richest saw their tax rate go up to 94 percent on taxable income over $200,000 (equivalent to $2.5 million in 2011). The theory was that people should be able to get by on $200,000. Tax rates came down somewhat in the 1960s and 1970s, but it wasn't until the 1980s that the tax bills of the wealthy really began to tumble after Congress converted the tax code into a boutique bank offering all sorts of products tailored just for them.

When Ronald Reagan took office in 1981, the top tax rate on salaries and wages was 50 percent; today it is 35 percent. The tax rate on unearned income—dividends and interest for example—was 70 percent. In 2012 it was 15 percent. The maximum tax rate on income from capital gains was 28 percent in 1980; in 2012 it was 15 percent.

Another dramatic change was the tax cut in 2003 for dividends paid to individuals by corporations. For much of recent history, dividends were taxed at a similar rate as salaries and wages. But before 1980, they were taxed at a higher rate than so-called earned income—money received in wages. The long-held theory was that people who worked for a living should not pay taxes at a higher rate than someone who lived on investment income. George W. Bush's Jobs and Growth Tax Relief Reconciliation Act of 2003 repealed that notion by slashing the maximum tax rate on dividends to 15 percent. This was a crowning moment in the annals of the great tax heist for the benefit of the wealthy. This one tax cut alone put billions of dollars into the pockets of the richest Americans. According to the Joint Committee on Taxation, which is required to prepare estimates of the implications of tax legislation passed by Congress, the dividend reduction cost the U.S. Treasury more than $100 billion over seven years. Politicians, economists, and media figures are fond of saying that more and more Americans own stock. President Bush later defended his 2003 tax cut on dividends by saying that "American families all across this country have benefited from

the tax cuts on dividends. . . . Half of American households—
that's more than 50 million households—now have some investment in the stock market."

Bush's claim is entirely misleading. While 50 percent of
Americans own *some* stock, often just a few shares, ownership
of shares and equities is concentrated in the hands of the
wealthiest Americans. They are the ones who receive substantial
dividends from stocks, and they are the ones who benefited
overwhelmingly from the dividend rate cut. That tax cut, along
with other Bush-era tax favors for the rich, is why the top
1 percent of Americans prospered to such an extreme during the
last decade.

Studies by economists Thomas Piketty and Emmanuel Saez
have concluded that "two-thirds of the nation's total income
gains from 2002 to 2007 flowed to the top U.S. households."
This is why the top 1 percent, they said, "held a larger share of
income in 2007 than at any time since 1928."

If Congress had not enacted these tax cuts, if Congress had
not opened new loopholes for its friends, and if Congress
had closed a few existing loopholes, we would not be having dis-
cussions about the dangers of the federal deficit. Tax cuts didn't
just fatten the bank accounts of rich people—they plunged the
nation deeper into the red. As for the folks in Washington who
made it all possible—mostly Republicans—they now want working people to cover the costs through reduced Social Security and
health care benefits at the same time that they want to guarantee

that the rich, the beneficiaries of all the largesse, will be insulated from any tax increases.

Any attempt to increase taxes would provoke stiff opposition from the elite, but when they whine about the taxes they pay, there are two things they never mention: in their grandparents' day, the rich paid taxes at twice the rate they do in the twenty-first century. Some don't come anywhere near paying even the maximum rate. By the IRS's own count, of the 400 tax return filers with the highest adjusted gross incomes in 2008, not one paid taxes at the top rate of 35 percent. It was the same for 2007 and the same for years before that. Those numbers underscore a long-time tax truism: if the top rate is 2 percent, some rich people will claim it is too high. Even the very rich who paid taxes did not come close to the top rate. For 30 of those 400 filers, their effective tax rate was under 10 percent. And for 101 of the top earners, the effective tax rate was between 10 and 15 percent.

Beyond the top 400, a whopping 18,783 individuals and families with incomes of more than $200,000 paid not one cent in federal income tax for 2008. That was up 1,782 percent from 1995, when only 998 individuals and families reported that they owed no income tax, according to IRS data. And that exponential growth occurred during a time when the people at the top of the economic pile seized more of the nation's overall wealth than at any time since the years leading up to the Great Depression.

Some high-income folks will threaten to pack up and leave the United States when they think taxes are too high. That obviously is everyone's right. But once that right is exercised, they should cease to enjoy any of the privileges that come with U.S. citizenship.

Corporations also will threaten to vote with their feet and move business operations to another country. That, too, is their choice. But they also should face a similar loss of U.S. benefits—like all the standard legal protections they enjoy courtesy of the taxes they should pay, but don't even pay now. Think patents, copyrights, and the American legal system, among others. Would Apple have achieved its lofty stock price absent such protections?

To fully appreciate the inequity of the U.S. tax system, visit your local bank and ask a teller to show you some Capital Gains dollar bills.

When you get a puzzled stare, ask for some Dividend dollar bills.

If there still isn't a hint of recognition, drop the big one: you would like to see a Carried Interest dollar bill.

If the teller still has a quizzical expression, just say that you will settle for some old-fashioned Work bills—the kind you get from your job as a store clerk or as a schoolteacher or as a carpenter.

You might think that a dollar is a dollar. After all, it can be used to buy an ice cream cone or pay your child's tuition or cover medical expenses. But to the IRS not all dollars are equal. Long ago, members of Congress, responding to the wishes of their well-heeled constituents, ordered the IRS to treat some dollars differently. This arrangement ensures preferential tax treatment for the privileged, including members of Congress, many of whom are millionaires. If all dollars were treated the same, as they should be, the deficit would disappear, with only a few adjustments in tax rates. But that would mean that the super-rich and the privileged would have to pay more taxes. It's not about to happen.

Among those who have benefited from having their own congressionally approved dollar bills are the men who run the hedge funds. Part of their earnings take the form of what the architects of tax language have labeled "carried interest." Because these earnings are performance-related, they are taxed at a much lower rate as capital gains, not as income. The government taxes a carried interest dollar at a maximum of 15 percent. Most people in America in regular salaried jobs pay taxes at a higher rate. But they don't speak the language of the privileged—people like the Republican presidential candidate Mitt Romney, who acknowledged that he pays taxes approaching 15 percent, thanks in part to carried interest, on income up to $42.6 million over two years. Most of us don't understand the incredible importance of carried interest, or even what it is. It's the kind of complex, murky term that has made the tax code such a field day for the rich and their lawyers. But the lesson of carried interest is clear: there is one dollar for the rich, and one much smaller dollar for the rest of us.

If hedge fund managers and others were required to pay taxes at the normal rate, it would generate tens of billions in additional tax revenue. It would also remove some egregious unfairness.

Philip Falcone, the billionaire creator of Harbinger Capital Partners, a New York City–based hedge fund, made a fortune betting against subprime mortgages before the collapse of the housing market. John Paulson, another hedge fund manager, made an even bigger fortune betting that subprime mortgages would be a loser. In short, two billionaire hedge fund managers made staggering sums betting that you would default on your mortgage and lose your house and that the financial institution holding your mortgage would collapse. In doing so, they were taxed at a much lower rate on that income than the rate applied to the salary you received, which went to pay the mortgage on the house you no longer have. How can that be right?

Falcone and Paulson are but two of this mushrooming breed of global financial buccaneers in private equity and hedge funds who have made huge amounts of money courtesy of Congress's largesse on the carried interest deduction. The riches that have come their way are financing lifestyles that average Americans cannot even fathom. If the fraternity were to bestow an award for flaunting that wealth, the hands-down winner would be Stephen Schwarzman, the CEO of Blackstone, the huge private equity fund.

Schwarzman's now-infamous multimillion-dollar sixtieth birthday party in New York City has long since passed into the annals of "the rich are different than us," but it is worth revisiting for what it says about their boldness and ability to turn aside any public policy that threatens their wealth.

Held at the famed Seventh Regiment Armory on Park Avenue on February 14, 2007, Schwarzman's birthday party attracted hundreds of the glitterati from New York and beyond. Arriving guests were ushered inside by a brass band and a contingent of children dressed in military uniforms. The cavernous armory, home to the most prestigious antiques show in America every year, was festooned with colorful banners and had been decorated to resemble the Schwarzmans' Park Avenue apartment. Copies of paintings from Schwarzman's art collection were mounted on the walls, and a huge portrait of Schwarzman himself, painted by the head of Britain's Royal Society of Portrait Painters, had been sent over from Schwarzman's apartment to greet arriving guests. "Dinner was served in a faux night club setting, with orchids and palm trees," according to the *Wall Street Journal.* Patti LaBelle sang "Happy Birthday," composer Marvin Hamlisch performed a number from *A Chorus Line,* and Rod Stewart sang for half an hour for a fee reported to be $1 million.

After stories of the party appeared in the media, legislation was introduced in the Senate to repeal the carried interest tax break that gave Schwarzman and his fellow private equity managers multimillion-dollar tax breaks on their personal income.

Hearings were held, and the giveaway was roundly condemned. But the proposal went nowhere. Behind the scenes, the leaders of private equity firms pumped millions of dollars into a lobbying campaign that scuttled the move to make them play by the same rules as everyone else.

When President Obama later proposed a similar reform, Schwarzman leveled an outrageous charge: "It's a war," Schwarzman told a nonprofit board. "It's like when Hitler invaded Poland in 1939."

Schwarzman later apologized for comparing the president to Hitler, but the repeal of the private equity loophole didn't go anywhere that time either. Game, set, match for private equity. And no surprise: the ruling class is now so powerful that it can brazenly flaunt its wealth—wealth it owes in part to middle-class taxpayers—at a shindig like Schwarzman's party without fear of losing its privileges.

As should be clear by now, Congress, at the direction of those at the top, has created two different tax systems: one for the wealthy and one for everyone else. America's founders, who were very well aware of how the aristocracy rigged the system to guarantee its own perpetuation, up to and including the king, would shudder. We all know the importance of luck in having wealthy parents. But under the twisted U.S. tax system, it's especially important for tax purposes. If you are among the privileged and your company rakes in billions of dollars over the years, essentially tax-free, the basis for those tax freebies may be passed along to the next generation.

Such is the case with Carnival Cruise Lines, a Miami-based company whose glitzy megaships have names like *Carnival Fantasy, Ecstasy, Elation,* and *Paradise.* Over the six years from 2005 to 2010, Carnival, the world's largest cruise carrier, racked up

$13 billion in profits. The company's tax bill for the six years? Chump change of $191 million. And that included U.S. income tax, foreign income tax, and local income tax. The overall tax rate came in at 1.4 percent. Carnival's ships may sail out of Miami and be inspected by the U.S. Coast Guard, but its finances hardly touch our shores. Middle America has not fared nearly so well, thanks to a Congress that likes to sock it to ordinary people, the same people who are and will be hammered even more as law-makers and the elite target them to be a scapegoat for the bal-looning deficits. While corporate profits have continued to climb, the wages of working people remain frozen in time. In 2008, ac-cording to IRS data, 10 million working individuals and fami-lies filed tax returns reporting incomes between $30,000 and $40,000. Their effective tax rate: 6.8 percent—nearly five times the Carnival rate.

This helps explain how members of the Arison family, who started Carnival, have held membership in that exclusive club of global billionaires for two decades.

Ted Arison was born in Tel Aviv in 1924 and moved to the United States in 1952. In 1972 he formed a joint venture to es-tablish a shipping business. His partner was Meshulam Riklis, who was born in Turkey but also grew up in Tel Aviv. Riklis, too, moved to the United States, where he eventually became an early-day corporate takeover artist, working alongside the leg-endary junk bond king Michael Milken.

The Arison-Riklis arrangement lasted only two years until Ari-son bought out Riklis in 1974. From that point on, he main-

tained tight control of what would become the company's flagship brand, Carnival Cruise Lines. He systematically added ships,
amenities like gambling, and passengers. Each of his ships was a
floating casino featuring slot machines, roulette, "Big Six" wheels,
and tables for craps and blackjack. In 1987 Arison took the company public, and a hefty chunk of the proceeds from the sale of
stock went to Arison personally. His take, according to U.S. Securities and Exchange Commission (SEC) records, was a special
dividend of $81 million.

Carnival has long been a master at avoiding U.S. income
taxes. The fine print in a document filed by Carnival with the
SEC allowed that:

> The company is not subject to United States corporate tax
> on its income from the operation of ships, and the com-
> pany does not expect such income to be subject to such tax
> in the future. This exemption from United States corporate
> income tax will remain in effect under current United
> States law for as long as the company retains its status as a
> controlled foreign corporation.

Even better for Arison and his family was yet another provision in the SEC public offering document that said: "The company intends to distribute dividends to all shareholders in at least
such amounts as are necessary to enable the principal shareholders to pay the income taxes imposed on them with respect to
those earnings."

Translation: whatever taxes Arison or his family incurred would be covered by a payment to them from the Carnival Corporation.

Imagine such a deal: when you receive your W-2 from your employer next January, ask if the company would write you a check to cover the taxes withheld from your paycheck! This perk, of course, doesn't exist for 99 percent of us.

Ted Arison renounced his U.S. citizenship in 1990 to further insulate himself personally from the U.S. income tax, and he returned to Israel. Years earlier, his son Micky, a fixture in Miami, had assumed day-to-day control of the business empire, which also includes the Miami Heat, the National Basketball Association team. The elder Arison died in 1999. Son Micky and daughter Shari inherited their father's tax freebies, meaning a second generation of the Arison family continues to enjoy the benefits of a company that pays only token taxes, thanks to a beneficent Congress.

Along the way, Micky and Shari also secured their very own slots on *Forbes* magazine's global list of billionaires. For 2012, the total is drawn from fifty-eight countries. He is number 223. She is number 288.

POOF! THE DISAPPEARING TAX ACT

Corporations, like the very wealthy, have also seen their taxes go down over the years. In 1952 corporate taxes accounted for 32 percent of the federal government's overall tax collections. The corporate share in 2011 was 7.9 percent. When World War II

started for the United States in 1941, corporate taxes amounted
to 1.9 percent of the nation's gross domestic product (GDP). By
war's end in 1945, that figured had gone up to 7.2 percent. It
would never reach that level again. In fact, during the first decade
of the twenty-first century, when the United States was waging
not one but two wars, in Iraq and Afghanistan, the ruling class
and their allies in Congress not only held corporate tax rates
down but forced them lower even as they continued a policy of
non-enforcement of the tax laws.

As a result, corporate tax collections added up to a meager
1 percent of GDP in 2009—the lowest level since the Great Depression. This at a time when corporate profits topped $1 trillion
for the fifth consecutive year—double what they were as recently
as the 1990s. Those who make the rules had achieved the perfect
formula: the more money a corporation rakes in, the lower its
U.S. tax bill. Underlying this formula is a condition that most
people recognize: in a global economy, higher profits do not mean
more jobs. More often than not, they mean just the opposite.

Further increasing the tax burden on the middle class, the
number of corporations that pay little or no corporate income
tax has exploded. They are large and small, closely controlled and
owned publicly. Their one common trait is that they operate in
multiple countries. Companies whose businesses are solely in the
United States are treated most unfairly compared to the multinationals. They often pay taxes at the maximum rate or close to
it, since they have few opportunities to move their cash around

the globe's assorted tax havens, unless they are willing to engage in flagrant tax avoidance, bordering on evasion, which is a crime.

The more prominent corporate tax avoiders have been publicly identified in the news media. The familiar names include General Electric Company (GE), which ranks number six on the current Fortune 500 list, its interests ranging from jet engines to financing, from health care to appliances. SEC documents show that in the three years from 2008 to 2010, GE reported no corporate tax owed in one year and in the other two years taxes well below the prevailing rate. The Boeing Company, the airplane manufacturer and defense contractor, has siphoned far more money out of your pockets and the pockets of other taxpayers by way of government contracts than it pays in taxes itself. In the three years from 2009 to 2011, the company reported owing no federal income tax. In 2011 Boeing ranked number three on the list of the largest government contractors at $8.4 billion.

Wells Fargo—one of the big banks that "originated, purchased, and securitized billions of dollars in home loans each year," in the words of a 2011 Senate report—helped bring down the economy and destroy the lives of millions of working people before it picked up a TARP (Troubled Asset Relief Program) bailout. For the years 2008 to 2010, Wells Fargo earned the coveted top spot on the list of twenty-five companies that avoided paying the most taxes. Its winning number: $17.96 billion in tax breaks, according to Citizens for Tax Justice (CTJ), a Washington public-interest group that compiles the rankings yearly.

Exxon Mobil Corporation, the global energy giant, came in at number six on the CTJ list at $4 billion off its tax bill. Actually, it was a little better than that. Exxon Mobil claimed a tax benefit of $838 million, while it paid $15.8 *billion* in income taxes to other countries. Wells Fargo Bank reported $49 billion in profits from 2008 to 2010. Like Exxon Mobil, it too received a tax benefit—of $651 million.

Boeing, Exxon Mobil, GE, and the others have lots of company. A study of corporate tax returns for the years 1998 to 2005 conducted by the Government Accountability Office (GAO), the investigative arm of Congress, found that in any given year the number of large, foreign-controlled domestic corporations that reported no income tax liability was sometimes as high as 72 percent. In short, seven of every ten big corporations operating in the United States under foreign ownership paid no taxes. As for large corporations owned by U.S. citizens, an astonishing 55 percent reported that they owed no federal income tax.

Another GAO study identified eight tax havens that were home to anywhere from 123 to 569 offshore subsidiaries of major corporations. In one instance, 372 subsidiaries were owned by just four corporations. Businesses establish foreign subsidiaries for reasons other than taxes, but the tax appeal is much stronger in some countries than others—like the Cayman Islands, where no direct tax is imposed. Hence, you may keep your money there and invest it around the world essentially tax-free. Mitt Romney maintains personal trusts in the Cayman Islands, a fact that became public after he released his tax returns during his presidential campaign.

The Caymans are home to far more corporations than they are to people. The islands have a population of 53,000. But 93,000 companies exist there, at least on paper. One five-story office building is the official address of more than 18,000 corporations. One of the more prolific Cayman Islands corporations in the 2008 GAO report was Citigroup, which boasted 427 subsidiaries in tax havens, with nearly 20 percent of them in the Caymans. That's par for the course for Citigroup. The company and its various affiliates have long contrived the use of secret bank accounts for Third World dictators, a strategy it pioneered.

Bank of America counted 115 subsidiaries in tax havens, with 59 of those in the Caymans. Bank of America and Citigroup, of course, were among the financial institutions that contributed to the economic trashing of the middle class and then shared in the government bailout for their handiwork.

It's one thing to escape payment of most federal income taxes. It's something else to extort tax favoritism. That's effectively what a group of U.S. multinational corporations are doing. Because they conduct business around the world and move money in and out of tax havens and other countries to secure the lowest possible rate, many stash their cash offshore rather than bring it home, where they would be obliged to pay taxes on it.

They will bring it back only if Washington will agree to a tax holiday. They want the 35 percent corporate tax rate waived and would like Washington to impose a onetime rate of, say, 5 percent. If Washington refuses to accommodate them, well, they will keep the money offshore and allow it to accumulate until a more pliable administration comes along. Or they might just take the money and invest it someplace else, like China. If you want to understand the differences between you and the ruling class, try that ploy with the IRS someday. Just tell them if they don't lower your tax rate you are going to move your money to another country.

The huge corporations that conduct business in multiple countries do pay income taxes in those countries, albeit at a much reduced rate. But the United States levies its income tax on the global income of U.S. corporations. It then allows a credit for taxes paid abroad. In theory, this means that U.S. global businesses should never pay less than 35 percent of their profits in income taxes—a sum shared by other countries and the United States. But when it comes to taxes, things are never as they seem. Google stirred up controversy when its overseas tax rate was shown to be 2.4 percent, according to a global study by *Bloomberg News.* The company claims write-offs for money moved around the tax havens of the world, so it never shows up as "income" on its U.S. tax returns.

So how much corporate cash is sitting abroad? Possibly as much as $2 trillion. That's *trillion.* Even at a tax rate of 25 percent, that would generate $375 billion in revenue, or the equivalent of all the taxes paid by everyone earning less than $100,000 a year—that is, all of Middle America and the working poor, more than 100 million individuals and families. This one issue illustrates why the corporate elite always win—and why Middle America always loses, why the future is so bleak. As companies lobby for legislation to give them a mammoth tax break, there is no one in power in the U.S. government to speak—and act—for working America to counterbalance corporate power.

While some in the GOP would prefer to include repatriation in a broad overhaul of the Internal Revenue Code, others don't want to wait. "Repatriation is an interim step that we can take to encourage businesses to bring investment back into our country," says Eric Cantor, the House majority leader. "Such a step adds capital that would otherwise go overseas directly into our economy which will help create jobs, investment, and growth." Many Democrats also have signed on to the cause, among them Barbara Boxer of California: "By bringing back the more than $1 trillion that's sitting overseas, we will create jobs, strengthen the economy, and reduce the deficit," says Boxer.

Neither Cantor nor Boxer, nor many others in Congress, have much concern for tax fairness. If they did, they'd oppose this giveaway to big business, which would reward a handful of American corporations at the expense of all other companies, most of them domestically based. More than 95 percent of U.S. corporations would not benefit from a tax holiday. Just as the tax code overflows with provisions that benefit wealthy individual taxpayers over average citizens, the holiday for overseas earnings rewards the largest corporations over smaller companies.

A coalition of small businesses, which always end up paying taxes at the highest rates, wrote Congress explaining the inequity of a tax holiday:

When powerful large U.S. corporations avoid their fair share of taxes, they undermine U.S. competitiveness, contribute to the national debt and shift more of the tax burden to domestic businesses, especially small businesses that create most of the new jobs. A transparent corporate tax system that assures all companies—large and small—pay for the services upon which our businesses, our customers, our workforce and our communities depend, would help restore the economic vitality and domestic job creation we all seek.

Nonetheless, the lobbying power, as always, rests with Big Business, which in this case has adhered to the rich tradition of giving its lobbying organization a name that means just the opposite of what the words suggest.

WIN America—a catchy acronym for "Working to Invest Now in America"—has very little to do with creating jobs, but a great deal to do with securing a tax break worth billions of dollars for its corporate clients.

Among those working on the WIN America campaign is SKDKnickerbocker, a public relations and political consulting firm that, by its own account, has "a track record of taking on the most difficult communication challenges—and helping our clients reach their goals." As the firm says on its website, "It is important to have a partner who understands how to strategically structure and deliver the right message on the right platform. It's your message, and we work with you to develop it through research and then help you implement it through a strategic communications plan, advertising, print and direct mail. The stakes have never been higher."

In the kind of coincidence that occurs all the time in Washington, a managing director in the SKDKnickerbocker office overseeing the WIN America project is a veteran political operative, Karen Olick, who helped Boxer win her first term as a U.S. senator from California in 1992 and then spent eleven years as Boxer's chief of staff. Another SKDKnickerbocker managing director in Washington is Anita Dunn, a senior adviser in President Obama's first presidential campaign and later White House interim communications director. Thus, while Obama pledges to make those at the top pay more taxes, one of his former top aides is working the other side of the street.

The onetime staff members to the people who make the laws, as well as the former members of Congress themselves who enacted legislation, are masterminding the campaign to return as much as $2 trillion to their corporate benefactors. Industries with the most to gain—pharmaceuticals, technology, and energy—have thrown their weight behind a massive $50 million (and counting) lobbying effort. Under the WIN America banner, executives of fifteen corporations signed a letter to President Obama and House and Senate leaders of the two parties, urging passage of legislation to bring home $1 trillion in profits free of significant U.S. taxes. Among the signers: Steve Ballmer, Microsoft CEO; Paul Jacobs, Qualcomm chairman and CEO; Ian Read, Pfizer president and CEO; Jim Rogers, Duke Energy chairman, president, and CEO; John Chambers, Cisco chairman and CEO; and Safra Catz, Oracle president and chief financial officer.

The letter contained a veiled threat of what might happen if Congress failed to act favorably on their request:

> In 2011 alone, U.S. companies have spent more than $150 billion of their overseas earnings on acquisitions of foreign companies or other foreign investments—money that otherwise could have been invested here at home to create new jobs and strengthen our economy. The simple truth is that the longer we wait, the more money will be spent overseas, and these foreign investments are unlikely to return to the U.S. even if our tax policies are changed to encourage domestic investment in the future.

These executives fully expect their companies to be given preferential treatment by the U.S. government. After all, they usually get what they ask for and they have been here before. In 2004 lawmakers enacted a tax holiday that allowed $312 billion back into the United States at a token tax rate of 5.25 percent—less than the rate actually paid by individuals and families earning $30,000 to $40,000. The only beneficiaries were the select corporations, their bottom lines, and their executives, who pocketed tens of millions in stock options. There was no surge in new hires. There was no dramatic increase in new plant construction. Essentially, there was no measurable benefit for the nation.

A 2011 study by the Permanent Subcommittee on Investigations of the Senate Committee on Homeland Security and Governmental Affairs concluded that just 843 corporations took advantage of the tax freebie. Those 843 companies represented a microscopic 0.015 percent of the 5,557,965 corporations that filed U.S. tax returns in 2004. Of the $312 billion brought home largely free of taxes, the Senate committee found that $157 billion, or half, "went to multinational corporations in just two industry sectors, the pharmaceutical and technology industries." In most cases, the money was channeled through corporate subsidiaries in tax havens that served little purpose other than to avoid the tax collector. The pharmaceutical giant Merck & Company brought back $16 billion, but to add insult to injury, the Senate committee found that, after bringing money back to the United States, Merck started the process all over again, stockpiling an additional $40 billion offshore in anticipation of another tax holiday at some point in the future.

Eli Lilly, another pharmaceutical company, brought $9.5 billion back to the United States, most of it from a holding company in Switzerland that, with its twelve subsidiaries, had a total of eighty-six employees. Some money came back through an investment holding company in the British Virgin Islands. It had no employees.

Oracle, which describes itself as "the world's largest enterprise software company and a leading provider of computer hardware products and services," brought back $3.3 billion the last time. The money came largely from an Irish subsidiary that had no physical office. It was designed, Oracle told the Senate committee, to "facilitate business operations outside of the United States."

When Senate committee staffers asked the repatriating companies if the subsidiaries sitting on the untaxed cash had ongoing operations, most said that they were holding companies "designed primarily to hold funds or facilitate the movement of funds among a network of foreign subsidiaries." But don't go looking for them. "A number of those tax haven subsidiaries," Senate investigators found, "had no physical office and few or no full time employees in the tax haven jurisdiction."

And that is how profits actually earned in the United States can be routed through shell companies in tax havens that impose minimal or no corporate income tax. Paul Egerman, a Boston entrepreneur, has no sympathy for the global businesses. "It is simply wrong," he says, "that a U.S.-based multinational company is able to report profits to their shareholders and losses to Uncle Sam."

THE UNITED STATES AS TAX HAVEN

One might almost feel sorry for American banks at the sight of all those dollars fleeing the United States for sunnier (and less taxed) bank accounts overseas. But any pity would be misplaced. Often the money ends up in a foreign branch of the same bank. Additionally, it is frequently replaced in the American branch by new money pouring into the banks from foreign corporations. Think of what's happening as a two-lane electronic superhighway. On one lane, trillions of dollars—and yes, that's trillions— are gushing out of the country and into and out of tax havens around the world. On the other lane, trillions of dollars are flooding into the United States—the world's newest, largest, and most secretive tax haven. The United States a tax haven? Don't our elected leaders bemoan the existence of tax havens like the Cayman Islands, Switzerland, Jersey and Guernsey in the Channel Islands, and the Isle of Man? They do indeed. But never confuse what Washington and Wall Street say with what either is really up to.

For years foreign investors have used the Internet to invite wealthy Americans to open secret accounts in tax haven countries, most with the clear goal of avoiding U.S. taxes. Now those invitations are urging wealthy people around the world to establish such accounts *in the United States.* Like this one by Connex International Services, headquartered in the United Kingdom, with a U.S. branch in Wilmington, Delaware:

> Many people do not realize the enormous tax benefits given to "non-resident aliens" making passive income in the United States, or earning income outside the United

States and simply using the USA as their own personal "offshore tax haven." The United States does not tax non-resident aliens for any interest income or dividend income derived from the United States. There is zero capital gains on profits from investments. There is zero tax on income earned outside the USA.

Connex says that investors don't even have to be immigrants to the United States to take advantage of U.S. tax laws. They just have to spend less than six months a year to qualify for all the tax-sheltered goodies. In language that would make any Caribbean tax promoter proud, Connex boasts that it "can also establish U.S. Limited Liability Companies (LLCs) which are very effective when you need to establish full service bank and brokerage accounts and a business presence in the USA while avoiding unnecessary tax liabilities."

So the United States, at the behest of its financial institutions, has morphed into a tax haven country. It goes unsaid, but obviously is understood by sophisticated foreign investors, that U.S. banks enjoy a unique relationship with the U.S. government and will get pretty much whatever they want. (Remember the trillion-dollar bailout of the banks and Wall Street, the very institutions that economically trashed tens of millions of working Americans, who were largely abandoned by the government?)

Does America's new status as a tax haven for foreigners mean that U.S. authorities have less interest in going after tax cheats who illegally park money offshore? The story of Bradley Birkenfeld would seem to suggest that.

Birkenfeld was born into the privileged life of a Boston-area neurosurgeon and his wife. In 1988 he graduated from Norwich University in the Green Mountains of Vermont, the first private military college in the United States. With a freshly minted economics degree, he returned to Boston and went to work in a series of low-level banking jobs, before heading off to Switzerland to secure an MBA at the American Graduate School of Business on the shores of Lake Geneva. After collecting his MBA, Birkenfeld began his real career in the wealth management field, where he could exploit his networking skills. In 2001 he moved from Barclays Bank to the venerable UBS, taking with him a prized client, Igor Olenicoff, a certified member of the Forbes directory of global billionaires. A Russian, Olenicoff had emigrated from the Soviet Union to the United States many years earlier, made a lot of money in California and Florida real estate, and divided his time between homes in those two states. Birkenfeld tended to Olenicoff's various financial needs, including, at one point, transferring money from UBS accounts to the New Haven Trust Company Ltd., a small private bank in Liechtenstein. The reason? Birkenfeld assured his Russian client that Liechtenstein had better secrecy laws than Switzerland.

In 2006 Birkenfeld resigned from UBS, but continued to provide offshore banking services to U.S. clients through a Swiss corporation with offices in Miami. He also continued to work with

Mario Staggl, who owned and operated New Haven Trust in Liechtenstein. Over the years, according to U.S. court documents, Staggl "devised, marketed and implemented tax evasion schemes" through the use of "Liechtenstein nominee entities, Liechtenstein banks, and Danish shell companies." On behalf of their tax-averse clients, Staggl and Birkenfeld routed money through phony companies and assorted tax haven countries to conceal income: standard fare in foreign tax havens.

But in 2007 Birkenfeld became concerned about what he was doing and approached the IRS seeking whistleblower status. If the IRS agreed, Birkenfeld would receive, in exchange for inside information on international tax fraud and the roles played by UBS and Swiss bankers generally, a percentage of the tax revenue ultimately recovered. For the IRS, this was a golden opportunity to do what had never been done before: unveil the inner workings of the legendary secret Swiss banking system, which featured untraceable cell phones, fake trusts, encrypted computers for bankers to use when they traveled around the United States signing up new clients, and the tactic of personally carrying checks back to Switzerland so as not to trigger a suspicious activity report by the Treasury Department.

It was all very cloak and dagger. On one occasion Birkenfeld had used a client's money to buy diamonds, stuffed them in a toothpaste tube, and brought the contraband into the United States, with Homeland Security and the IRS none the wiser. Bankers would meet clients at prestigious public events like the

NASDAQ tennis tournament and Art Basel Miami Beach, where more than 250 leading galleries from around the world showcase the works of 2,000 artists of the twentieth and twenty-first centuries. In 2004 alone, 32 Swiss bankers came to the United States and met with clients about 3,800 times. No matter the event, all of those meetings had the same unifying feature: rich Americans with money to conceal from the IRS.

Birkenfeld also provided inside information to the Securities and Exchange Commission and the Permanent Subcommittee on Investigations of the Senate Committee on Homeland Security and Governmental Affairs.

In large part because of Birkenfeld's information about his former employer, UBS agreed to pay $780 million to the U.S. Treasury to settle claims that it had helped cheat the United States out of tax revenue. Igor Olenicoff, the California and Florida real estate developer, paid $52 million in back taxes, fines, and penalties. He added another layer of intrigue to the tax evasion scheme by saying that one of the sham companies was actually an entity that Russia's president at the time, Boris Yeltsin, had set up to make foreign investments.

As for Birkenfeld, the very same Justice Department that said in court documents that he had provided "substantial assistance" that was "timely, significant, useful, truthful, complete, and reliable" sent him to the slammer. Indicted for conspiring to help people hide money from the tax collector, Birkenfeld pleaded guilty and was sent to prison for forty months. Why the Justice

Department chose to jail an informant who helped the United States recoup billions of dollars in concealed taxes and helped disclose the existence of more than 20,000 secret American offshore accounts holding nearly $20 billion is uncertain. What is clear is that the Justice Department sent an unmistakable message to future whistleblowers: turn in a list of tax cheats and it's quite likely that you—not the tax law violators—will go to prison.

To date, few have. In fact, most of the cheats were given amnesty if they agreed to pay up. But the vast majority of Americans who held the secret UBS accounts have never been identified. UBS itself and several of its executives all just paid fines. As for Mario Staggl, he simply disappeared into the mists of foreign tax havens, never to be seen by U.S. authorities, who declared him a fugitive. Birkenfeld's boss, who presided over the global tax fraud scam, fared even better. Martin Liechti pleaded the Fifth Amendment when he was called to testify before Congress. After being detained for a few months, he was allowed to return to Switzerland. He was never charged with a crime.

The Justice Department's handling of Birkenfeld stirred indignation among tax professionals, the news media, and the whistleblower community. It's generally understood that whistleblowers in any field often enter the courthouse with less than clean hands. But it's also generally understood that the good they can accomplish far outweighs their personal transgressions. *Tax Notes,* a highly respected weekly publication on federal taxation, proclaimed Birkenfeld its "2009 Tax Person of the Year" for successfully disclosing "what goes on in the wealth protection units of the world's major banks." The *Atlantic* called the prosecution one of "the five *worst* law-related moves by the Obama White House and Justice Department." And *Time* asserted that "almost no one in the U.S. government would deny that Birkenfeld was absolutely essential to its landmark tax-evasion case against Swiss banking giant UBS."

The sentence was handed down on August 21, 2009, in the U.S. District Court in Fort Lauderdale, Florida. Six days later, President Obama, on vacation with his family at Martha's Vineyard, set off to play several hours of golf with friends. Among his golfing partners was Robert Wolf, the head of UBS's American operations, an early financial supporter of Obama and one of his major bundlers of campaign contributions. Wolf continues to fill that role, in addition to stopping by the White House for occasional dinners and other gatherings.

CHAPTER 6

THE END
OF
RETIREMENT

O f all the statistics that show how the rules are changing for middle-class Americans, here is one of the most alarming: since 1985, corporations have killed 84,350 pension plans—each of which promised secure retirement benefits to dozens or hundreds or even thousands of men and women.

Corporations offer many explanations and excuses for why they are cutting down a vital safety net for Americans, but it all comes down to money. The money saved by not funding employee pensions now goes for executive salaries, dividends, or some pet project of a company's CEO. Congress went along and even compounded the betrayal by pretending that the change was in employees' best interest.

What this means is that fewer and fewer Americans will have enough money to take care of themselves in their later years. As with taxes and trade, Congress has been pivotal in granting favors to the most powerful corporations. Lawmakers have written pension rules that encourage businesses to underfund their retirement plans or switch to plans less favorable to employees. These rules deny workers the right to sue to enforce retirement promises. Lawmakers have also written bankruptcy regulations to allow corporations to scrap the health insurance coverage they promised to employees who retired early—including workers who were forced into early retirement. Congress has enacted legislation that adds to the cost of retirement. One by one, policies that once afforded at least the possibility of a secure retirement to many seniors have been undermined or destroyed, while at the same time Congress has allowed corporations to repudiate lifetime-benefit agreements.

Pensions were once an integral part of the American dream, a pledge by corporations to their employees: for your decades of work, you can count on retirement benefits. In return for lower earnings in the present, you were promised compensation in the future when you retired. Not everyone had a pension, but from the 1950s to the 1980s, the number of workers who did rose steadily—until 1985. Since then, more and more companies have walked away from pensions, reneging on their promise to their employees and leaving millions at risk.

Before today's workers reach retirement age, decisions by Congress favoring moneyed interests will drive millions of older

Americans—most of them women—into poverty, push millions more to the brink, and turn the golden years into a time of need for everyone but the affluent.

For all of this you can thank the rule makers of Wall Street and Washington who have colluded to rewrite the rules on retirement in ways that will harm millions of middle-class Americans for decades. Here is what they have done:

- In addition to the 84,350 pension plans killed by corporations since 1985, companies have frozen thousands of other plans, meaning that new employees are barred from participating or benefit levels are frozen, or both. Freezing a pension plan is often the first step toward eliminating it.

- The congressionally touted replacements for pensions—401(k) plans—have insufficient holdings to provide a serious retirement benefit. This even though millions will be depending on them.

- As companies have killed or curtailed pensions for employees, executive pensions have soared, largely because they are based on executives' compensation—which has ballooned in recent decades.

- At some companies the only employees who have pensions are the corporation's executives.

- The 401(k) plans promoted by corporations and Congress that have replaced pensions as the main retirement plan for many employees are uninsured, and they are less secure and cost more to administer than traditional pensions, but they have provided a windfall of fees for Wall Street.

- Workers' pensions are insured by the federal Pension Benefit Guaranty Corporation (PBGC), but the agency faces mounting deficits, raising the question of whether it will be able to fully honor all pensions that may be defaulted by private companies in the future.

The result of these changes is that America has devolved into a land of two separate and decidedly unequal retirement systems—one for the have-mores and another for the have-lesses, whose numbers are exploding. Those who have less aren't just the poor, whose later years have always been a struggle; now they include large numbers of the middle class—men and women, individuals and families, who once eagerly awaited retirement, but now fear what those years will bring. People like Kathy Coleman of Ave Maria, Florida.

Like millions of others who once looked forward to that time, retirement isn't on Kathy's radar. She didn't expect this. Kathy grew up in St. Clair Shores, Michigan, the daughter of a tool and die engineer. She graduated from Wayne State University in Detroit with majors in art and interior design. She married, had two sons, and started a career in interior design. After her sons were grown and she was single again, she moved to Florida and went to work as the cultural and social events director at the exclusive

Polo Club of Boca Raton. She arranged concerts, coordinated speakers and excursions for members, prepared the annual budget and monthly reports, and helped create the club's annual calendar of events.

In 2005, intrigued by a new town that Domino's pizza founder Tom Monaghan was building near Naples on the west coast of Florida, she relocated, taking a job as conference director for Legatus, an organization of wealthy Catholic business leaders that Monaghan had founded. She wrote marketing copy and articles for the Legatus website and helped coordinate the group's conferences, including an annual pilgrimage to Rome for an audience with the pope. She bought a new home in the community of Ave Maria, near the university of the same name, which Monaghan had also founded. On a quiet street, the three-bedroom house made an attractive place for her sons and their families to visit. It would also be a good place to retire.

Two years and eight months later, Kathy and some of her coworkers lost their jobs at Legatus. It was a blow that caught them by surprise. One distraught employee later committed suicide. Kathy brushed up her résumé and began looking for work, assuming that with her years of experience in a wide range of jobs, it would be only a matter of time before she found one. But there was nothing. To make her mortgage payment and meet other expenses, she withdrew savings and started tapping into her 401(k). At a time when she would have liked to have been putting money away for retirement—she was in her sixties—she had to dip into her nest egg just to keep a roof over her head. At one point she worked at three part-time jobs and took an online course to become a real estate sales associate. She also organized a career counseling class at a local church to provide practical tips and moral support for others like herself.

With her financial situation growing increasingly dire, she ultimately took a job behind the deli counter of a grocery store. The woman who had helped arrange visits to the pope was now slicing ham and cheese. She learned how to close the store for the night—how to take apart and clean the slicers, tidy up cabinets and coolers, and disassemble the metal over floor drains so they could be mopped. "I hadn't worked in anything like this since I was in my teens," she said. Eventually she qualified for the company's health plan, and in her first year she got a raise—a fifteen-cent-an-hour increase that put her up to $10.40 an hour.

If things had worked out differently, Kathy, sixty-three, might be thinking of retirement. Instead, simply holding on to her house is her most important priority. She renegotiated the mortgage and lowered the monthly payment with a forty-year mortgage. Unlike earlier generations of Americans who often left their debt-free homes to their children as an asset, Kathy will never be able to do that. Instead of saving in her later years and retiring the mortgage, she will be making payments to her bank as long as she lives if she stays in her house. Even after renegotiating her mortgage, money is still tight because her earnings are only one-third of what they once were. Having pulled money out of her 401(k), and being in no position to replenish it from her modest earnings, Kathy is just trying to get by while she continues to look for a job in which she can use her talents and experience. In the meantime, she's focused on the present: "I'm not living in the future anymore."

A few miles west of Kathy, in the wealthy seaside town of Naples, retirement looks very different to Bruce Sherman.

Sherman was a money manager who headed Private Capital Management, a Naples-based investment firm that caters to wealthy individuals. He made a lot of money over the years for his clients and himself, but his last big deal had lasting repercussions.

He was the money manager who in 2006 brought down Knight-Ridder, the nation's second-largest newspaper chain, which included the *Philadelphia Inquirer,* the *Miami Herald,* and the *San Jose Mercury News.* After gaining control of 19 percent of Knight-Ridder's stock, Sherman in 2005 demanded changes in the company's management, and when the response of company leaders didn't satisfy him, he decided to sell off all the shares he controlled.

But Sherman controlled such a large bloc of stock that if he dumped it into the market, its value would plummet. To preserve Private Capital Management's investment, Knight-Ridder had to be sold outright, through auction or otherwise. So Sherman decided "to bully the company into putting itself up for sale," according to the *American Journalism Review.*

To the surprise of its employees and the journalism world, Knight-Ridder caved and sold the company for $6.5 billion. The buyer was a smaller chain, McClatchy Newspapers, which in turn sold off a number of former Knight-Ridder papers to help offset the purchase price. The sale set off a chain reaction as investors fled the field, dumping their holdings in other newspaper stocks.

Every newspaper in the former Knight-Ridder chain has suffered greatly since Sherman's brief foray into the newspaper business. The troubles affecting former Knight-Ridder properties are part of an industry-wide trend that has hit all newspapers in the Internet era. But Sherman's acquisition of a large bloc of the company's stock on behalf of his clients served to drive up the company's stock price in excess of its value and was a contributing factor to the papers' later weaknesses in dealing with debt. Every former Knight-Ridder paper has gone through layoff after layoff, killed pensions, frozen benefits, mandated unpaid furloughs, or taken other harsh measures to try to remain viable. To be sure, newspapers had financial problems before Sherman, and they still do, but the run-up in the debt of Knight-Ridder papers that he provoked has saddled them with huge liabilities that have compounded their problems.

None of that concerns Sherman. He retired from Private Capital in 2009. This gave him more time to play golf and spend time with his grandchildren, he told a local reporter. It has also given him time for charitable events. One of his interests is the annual Naples Winter Wine Festival, which raises money for a local foundation to support programs for underprivileged and at-risk children. One of the highlights of the Naples social season, the festival often imports famous wine experts and notable chefs to entertain the wealthy attendees. Sherman and his third wife, Cynthia, were cochairs of the 2011 festival.

When not on the golf course or at a charitable event, Sherman can be found in his 12,050-square-foot penthouse at the Regent, a luxury high-rise condominium overlooking the blue waters of the Gulf of Mexico. He and Cynthia purchased the place for $9.5 million in 2003. Though it had been built only the year before, they called in a decorator who had worked with Steven Spielberg to spruce it up, according to local press accounts. The Regent has about everything one could want in a gated community: guest suites, an auto-spray car wash, a beachfront pool, and massage and exercise rooms. In his spacious penthouse, Sherman told a local reporter that he'd set aside one room for a special purpose: an office to manage his investments.

TURNING BACK THE CLOCK

For many Americans, the changes that would affect their retirement years arrived by stealth. The number of Americans covered by guaranteed pensions had risen steadily from 1950 to 1980: 10.3 million in 1950; 23 million in 1960; 35 million in 1970. By 1980, a total of 28 percent of the private workforce was covered by a defined benefit pension plan. This was the gold standard for retirement because a pension plan guaranteed retirees a fixed income for life.

But then Wall Street and corporate America decided that enough was enough: deeming pensions too costly for corporations and their stockholders, they began to kill pensions and shift employees into cheaper plans that paid employees less money.

From a peak of 112,000 defined-benefit plans that provided retirees with a guaranteed monthly income in 1985, the number plunged to 27,650 in 2011. By then, only 3 percent of private workers were covered solely by such plans.

More significantly, virtually no companies are creating these plans anymore, and only a few provide them to new employees. Fortune 500 companies are among those killing or freezing their defined-benefit plans by the score. In 1998 a total of 67 percent of the top one hundred Fortune 500 companies offered defined-benefit plans. By 2010 the figure had plunged to 17 percent, according to Towers Watson, the global consulting firm. Typical of the attitude toward pensions was Hewlett-Packard, long one of the most admired U.S. companies, which pulled the plug on guaranteed pensions for new workers. A spokesman said the company had concluded that "pension plans are kind of a thing of the past." In that, Hewlett-Packard was merely part of a corporate trend.

Major companies that have restricted their defined-benefit plans in some manner include Anheuser-Busch, Caterpillar Inc., CIGNA, DuPont, Kimberly-Clark, Kraft Foods, Motorola, R. R. Donnelley & Sons, Sunoco, and 3M. The nation's largest employer, Walmart, does not offer such pensions. At the current pace, human resource offices will turn out the lights in their defined-benefit section in the next few years. At that point, individuals will assume all the risks for their own retirement.

The shift away from guaranteed pensions was encouraged by Congress, which structured pension and retirement plan legislation in a way that invited corporations to abandon their defined-benefit plans in favor of defined-contribution plans—increasingly 401(k)s—in which employees set aside a fixed sum of money toward retirement. Many companies also contribute to these plans, but some don't. In either case, the contributions will never be enough to match the certain and long-term income from a defined-benefit plan. What's more, once the money runs out, that's it. If people live longer than expected, get stuck with unanticipated expenses, or suffer losses of other once-promised benefits, they will have little besides their Social Security to sustain them.

The move out of pensions and into 401(k)s was an intentional strategy to substantially reduce corporate costs. It was sold as a plus for employees, as part of what former President George W. Bush referred to often as the "ownership society" in which people would take charge of their own finances and all other phases of their economic lives and not depend on other parties to possibly dictate their financial future. Bush's Treasury secretary, John Snow, was an especially avid proponent: "I think we need to be concerned about pensions and the security that employees have in their pensions," Snow told a congressional committee in 2004.

"And I think we need to encourage people to save and become part of an ownership society, which is very much a part of the president's vision for America."

Of course, it's much easier to own a piece of America when you have a pension like Snow's. When he stepped down as head of CSX Corporation—operator of the largest rail network in the eastern United States—to take over Treasury, Snow was given a lump-sum pension of $33.2 million. It was based on forty-four years of employment at CSX. Unlike most people, who must work for forty-four years to receive a pension based on forty-four years of service, Snow was employed at CSX for just twenty-six years. The additional eighteen years of his CSX employment history were fictional, a parting gift from the company's board of directors.

At the same time as corporate executives are paid retirement dollars for years they never worked, hapless employees lose supplemental retirement benefits for a lifetime of actual work. Betty Moss was one of thousands of workers at Polaroid Corporation—the maker of instant cameras and film then based in Waltham, Massachusetts—who gave up 8 percent of their salary to underwrite an employee stock ownership plan, or ESOP. It was created to thwart a corporate takeover and "to provide a retirement benefit" to Polaroid employees to supplement their pension, the company pledged. It didn't happen. Slow to react to the digital revolution, Polaroid began to lose money in the 1990s. From 1995 to 1998, the company suffered $359 million in losses. As its balance sheet deteriorated, so did its stock price, including shares in the ESOP.

In October 2001, Polaroid sought bankruptcy protection. By then, Polaroid's shares were nearly worthless, having plummeted from $60 in 1997 to less than the price of a Coke in October 2001. During that period, employees were forbidden to unload their stock, based on laws approved by Congress. But what employees weren't allowed to do at a higher price, the company-appointed trustee could do at the lowest possible price—without even seeking the workers' permission. Rather than wait for a possible return to profitability through restructuring, the trustee decided that it was "in the best interests" of the employees to sell the ESOP shares. They went for nine cents. Just like that, the $300 million retirement nest egg of six thousand Polaroid employees was vaporized. Many lost between $100,000 and $200,000.

Betty Moss spent thirty-five years at Polaroid, beginning as a file clerk out of high school, then working her way through college at night and eventually rising to be senior regional operations manager in Atlanta. "It was the kind of place people dream of working at," she said. "I can honestly say I never dreaded going to work. It was just the sort of place where good things were always happening." One of those good things was supposed to be the ESOP, touted by the company as a plan that "forced employees to save for their retirement," as Betty recalled. "Everybody went for it. We had been so conditioned to believe what we were told was true." Once Polaroid entered bankruptcy,

Betty and her retired coworkers learned a bitter lesson—that they had no claim on benefits they had worked all their lives to accumulate. Although the federal PBGC agreed to cover most of their basic pensions, the rest of their benefits were canceled—not only the ESOP accounts but also their retiree health care and severance packages.

The retirees, who were generally well educated and financially savvy, organized to try to win back some of what they had lost by petitioning the bankruptcy court, which would decide how to divide the company's assets among creditors. But Polaroid's management undercut the employees' effort. Rather than file for bankruptcy in Boston, near the corporate offices, the company took its petition to a bankruptcy court in Wilmington, Delaware, that had developed a reputation for favoring corporate managers. There Polaroid's management contended that the company was in such terrible financial shape that the only option was to sell rather than reorganize. The retirees protested, arguing that Polaroid executives were undervaluing the business so that the company could ignore its obligations to retirees and sell out to private investors.

The bankruptcy judge ruled in favor of the company. In 2002 Polaroid was sold to One Equity Partners, an investment firm with a special interest in financially distressed businesses. (One Equity was a unit of Bank One Corporation, now part of JPMorgan Chase.) Many retirees believed that the purchase price of $255 million was only a fraction of Polaroid's value, and there is evidence to support that view: the new owners financed their purchase, in part, with $138 million of Polaroid's own cash.

Employees did not leave bankruptcy court empty-handed. They all got something in the mail. Betty Moss will never forget the day hers arrived. "I got a check for $47," she recalled. She had lost tens of thousands of dollars in ESOP contributions, health benefits, and severance payments. She and the rest of Polaroid's other six thousand retirees were being compensated with $47 checks. "You should have heard the jokes," she said. "'How about we all meet at McDonald's and spend our $47?'"

Any doubt as to how badly employees had been cheated by the company and the bankruptcy court was quickly dispelled when Polaroid emerged from court protection. Under a new management team headed by Jacques Nasser, former chairman of Ford Motor Company, Polaroid returned to profitability almost overnight. Little more than two years after the company came out of bankruptcy, One Equity sold it to a Minnesota entrepreneur for $426 million in cash. The new managers, who had received stock in the postbankruptcy Polaroid, walked away with millions of dollars. Nasser got $12.8 million for his 1 million shares. Other executives and directors also were rewarded for their efforts. Rick Lazio, a four-term Republican from West Islip, New York, who gave up his House seat for an unsuccessful Senate run against Hillary Rodham Clinton in 2000, collected $512,675 for a brief stint as a director—an amount nearly twice the $282,000 paid to all six thousand retirees. The $12.08 a share that the new managers received for little more than two years of work was 134 times the nine cents a share handed out earlier to lifelong workers.

Bankruptcy court's shunting aside Polaroid's workers in favor of the company's executives and new owners was all too typical of how other institutions also treat ordinary citizens on retirement matters. Washington has a long history of catering to special interests on pension legislation and regulations, dating back to 1964 when the Studebaker Corporation collapsed, junking the promised pensions of four thousand workers not yet eligible for retirement.

For years the carmaker had published brochures spelling out its promise to employees: "You may be a long way from retirement age now. Still, it's good to know that Studebaker is building up a fund for you, so that when you reach retirement age you can settle down on a farm, visit around the country or just take it easy, and know that you'll still be getting a regular monthly pension paid for entirely by the company."

It took Congress ten years to react to Studebaker's betrayal by writing the Employee Retirement Income Security Act (ERISA) of 1974. It established minimum standards for private retirement plans and created the Pension Benefit Guaranty Corporation to guarantee them. President Gerald Ford hailed the measure when he signed it into law that Labor Day: "This legislation will alleviate the fears and the anxiety of people who are on the production lines or in the mines or elsewhere, in that they now know that their investment in private pension funds will be better protected."

The biggest winners under the bill weren't working Americans, however, but money men. Congress wrote the law so broadly that it allowed corporate raiders to dip into pension funds and remove cash set aside for workers' retirement. During the 1980s, that's exactly what a cast of corporate raiders, speculators, Wall Street buyout firms, and company executives did with a vengeance, walking away with an estimated $21 billion earmarked for workers' retirement pay. The raiders insisted that they took only excess assets that weren't needed.

Among the pension buccaneers: Meshulam Riklis, the one-time partner of Carnival Cruise founder Ted Arison. A takeover artist, Riklis skimmed millions from several companies, including the McCrory Corporation, the former retail fixture of Middle America that is now gone; and the late Victor Posner, the Miami Beach corporate raider who siphoned millions of dollars from more than half a dozen different companies, including Fischbach Corporation, a New York electrical contractor that he drove to the edge of extinction. Those two raiders alone raked off about $100 million in workers' retirement dollars—all perfectly legal, courtesy of Congress. By the time billions of dollars were gone and the public outcry so loud that even Congress could not ignore it, lawmakers in 1990 rewrote the rules and imposed an excise tax on money removed from pension funds. The raids slowed to a trickle.

During those same years, the PBGC published an annual list of the fifty most underfunded pension plans. In spotlighting corporations that had fallen behind in their contributions, the agency hoped to prod companies to keep current. Corporations hated the list. They maintained that the PBGC's methodology did not reflect the true financial condition of their pension plans. After all, as long as the stock market went up, the pension plans would be adequately funded. Congress agreed with this specious reasoning and in 1994, to please corporate America, voted to keep the data on the underfunded pensions of individual corporations a secret.

When the PBGC killed its top fifty list, David M. Strauss, then the agency's executive director, explained, "With full implementation of [the 1994 pension law], we now have better tools in place." PBGC officials were so bullish about those "better tools," including provisions to levy higher fees on companies that ignored their commitments to their employees, that they predicted that underfunded pension plans would become a thing of the past. As a story in the *Los Angeles Times* put it, "PBGC officials said the act nearly guarantees that large underfunded plans will strengthen and the chronic deficits suffered by the pension guaranty organization will be eliminated within 10 years."

The prediction was wildly off. Instead, pension deficits soared and ten years later the deficit was $23.5 billion. Since the PBGC no longer publishes its top fifty list, anyone looking for remotely comparable information must sift through voluminous company reports to the SEC or the Labor Department, where pension-plan finances are recorded, or turn to independent reports, such as one compiled in 2011 by UBS that identifies twenty-five of the most underfunded pension plans. The names were familiar: Ford Motor Company ($11.4 billion); Whirlpool Corporation ($1.5 billion); Lockheed Martin Corporation ($10.4 billion); United States Steel Corporation ($1.9 billion); and Raytheon Company ($4 billion). All told, according to Credit Suisse, publicly traded companies in 2011 were confronting a combined pension short-fall of $458 billion.

In reality, the deficits in many cases are worse than the published data suggest, which becomes evident when bankrupt corporations dump their pension plans on the PBGC. Time after time, the agency has discovered, the gap between retirement holdings and pensions owed is much wider than the companies reported to stockholders or employees. For example, the giant Cleveland steelmaker LTV Steel Corporation reported that its plan for hourly workers was about 80 percent funded, but when it was turned over to the PBGC, there were assets to cover only 52 percent of benefits—a shortfall of $1.6 billion that the PBGC had to assume.

How can this be? Thanks to the way Congress writes the rules, pension accounting has a lot in common with Enron accounting, but with one difference: it's legal. By adjusting the arcane formulas used to calculate pension assets and obligations, corporate accountants can transform a drastically underfunded system into what appears to be a financially healthy plan, even inflate a company's profits and push up its stock price. Ethan Kra, chief actuary of Mercer Human Resources Consulting, once put it this way: "If you used the same accounting for the operations side [of a corporation] that is used on pension funds, you would be put in jail."

The PBGC lists of deadbeat pension funds served another purpose. They were an early-warning signal of companies in trouble—a sign often ignored or denied by the companies. "Somehow, if companies are making progress toward an objective that's consistent with [the PBGC's], then I think it's counterproductive to be exposed on this public listing," complained Gary Millenbruch, executive vice president of Bethlehem Steel, a perennial name on the top fifty.

Time proved Millenbruch wrong. The early warnings about Bethlehem's pension liabilities were right on target. When Bethlehem Steel later filed for bankruptcy, the PBGC found that its pension plans were short $3.7 billion. The company that was once America's second-largest steelmaker no longer exists. Contrary to the assertions of company executives, PBGC officials, and members of Congress, one company after another on the 1990 top fifty disappeared, many offloading their unfunded pensions on the PBGC.

Having seen how easy it is to unload a pension plan, more and more corporations are trying to do just that. In what threatened to be the largest company abandonment of its workers, AMR, the parent of American Airlines, filed for bankruptcy protection in November 2011 and asked a federal judge for permission to kill four pension plans covering 130,000 American workers and retirees.

The company asked that the PBGC assume responsibility for paying benefits to American's retirees. If approved, the plan would have cost American's retirees $1 billion in lost benefits because of caps imposed by Congress on the amount that PBGC can pay individual retirees.

After years of the PBGC rolling over to accommodate pension-killing corporations, the agency's new director, Joshua Gotbaum, decided to make a stand on American's plans, warning the airline that before it took such a "drastic action as killing the pension plans of 130,000 employees and retirees, it needs to show there is no better alternative. Thus far, they have failed to provide even the most basic information to decide that."

In what has to be chalked up as a modest victory for workers, American backed down from its plan to terminate all pensions and announced that it would instead freeze them. The details of what that may ultimately mean are not clear at this stage, other than that the plans will be preserved—at least in a reduced form. The issue is not likely to be fully resolved until American exits bankruptcy sometime in the future.

American was but the latest large airline attempting to jettison its employee pension plans. In the last decade, four big carriers— United, US Airways, Delta, and TWA—walked away from their employee plans and shifted the responsibility to pay retirement benefits from themselves to the PBGC.

When the PBGC takes over a retirement plan, it covers retirement checks up to a fixed amount—$55,000 in 2011. But it will only continue to do this until the agency runs out of money, a distinct possibility given its looming liabilities. The PBGC's financial position has rapidly deteriorated. In 2000 the agency operated with a $10 billion surplus. By the end of 2011, that had flipped to a $26 billion deficit—the highest in PBGC's thirty-seven-year history.

The Government Accountability Office (GAO) says that the PBGC's insurance funds are at "high risk" and the agency faces increasing challenges to meet its obligations. "PBGC's premium base has been shrinking as the number of defined benefit pension plans and active plan participants has declined rapidly," GAO said in 2010. With so many plans being canceled, the number of companies that pay premiums to PBGC has dropped precipitously; by 2011, only half as many companies paid premiums as fifteen years ago.

PAYING THE PRICE

The ease with which companies can eliminate or reduce their pension obligations is taking a toll on workers. Forty-nine-year-old Robin Gilinger, a United flight attendant for twenty-five years, is very worried. Before United entered bankruptcy, she had been promised a monthly retirement check of $2,184. Because of givebacks arising from the bankruptcy, that's down to $1,082, or $12,884 a year—a poverty-level income even before inflation takes its toll in coming years. Though she has a few years before she could take early retirement, she wonders if even the reduced benefit will be there. Her husband lost his pension in a corporate takeover. Like many Americans, Robin is not sure she'd be able to take early retirement even if it were an option, given how small the benefit would be. The dream of early retirement, once such a motive force in the middle class, is gone for almost everyone these days. Robin, who lives with her husband and teenage daughter in Mount Laurel, New Jersey, has concerns that mirror those of middle-class Americans everywhere. "It's scary. What if something happened to my husband or if I got disabled?" she asks. "Then I'm looking at nothing. Above all, what's frustrating is that we were told we were going to get our pension and we're not. The senior flight attendants, the ones who've worked thirty years, they're worried how they're going to survive."

Robin believes the government did a poor job of looking out for United employees. "Our pensions were unfairly taken," she said. Since the United bankruptcy, the company has done well, she said, and even remitted payments to PBGC, but she and her fellow workers are still going to receive less. "This was security for us and now that security is gone," she said. "I think the future just means working a lot harder for less."

Each time the PBGC takes on another failed pension plan, it makes the pension insurance program more expensive for the businesses that remain. That in turn prompts other companies to unload their plans. The PBGC receives no tax money. Its revenue comes from investment income and premiums that corporations pay on their insured workers. As a result, soundly managed companies with solid retirement plans are compelled to pick up the costs for plans in mismanaged companies as well as in those that just want to eliminate their employee benefits.

If the PBGC were to run out of money, the agency could require a multibillion-dollar taxpayer bailout. The last time that happened was during the 1980s and '90s, when another government insurer, the Federal Savings and Loan Insurance Corporation (FSLIC), was unable to keep up with a thrift industry spinning out of control. The federal government eventually spent $124 billion. Unlike the FSLIC, which was backed by the U.S. government, the PBGC is not. That means that Congress could turn its back on the retirement crash if it chose, a distinct possibility given the budget-cutting obsession of Capitol Hill deficit hawks whose own pensions are guaranteed by taxpayers. By the agency's estimate, that would translate into a 90 percent reduction in the pensions it currently pays—so retirees covered by the agency would receive no more than ten cents for every dollar that has been promised them.

At the heart of the retirement scenario engineered by the ruling class that will leave millions of Americans with far less than they will need in their later years is the now-ubiquitous 401(k). Just over three decades old, 401(k)s are corporate America's and Washington's answer to the pension. There is nothing wrong with 401(k)s as such if they are used as tax-sheltered savings plans or as a supplement in retirement, but as the principal retirement benefit for most Americans they fall hopelessly short.

To begin with, 401(k)s were never supposed to take the place of pensions. They were created in 1978 as a tax break given by Congress to corporate executives who wanted to defer part of their salaries and cut their tax bills. At the time, federal income tax rates were much higher for upper-income individuals—the top rate was 70 percent. (Today, as we discussed in Chapter 5, it's half that.) It wasn't until several years later that companies began to make 401(k)s available to most employees. Even then, the idea was to encourage saving and supplement retirement, not to create a substitute for pensions. By 1985, assets in 401(k)s had risen to $91 billion as more companies adopted plans, but that was still only about one-tenth of what had been set aside in guaranteed pension plans.

All that changed rapidly as corporations discovered they could fatten their bottom lines by shifting workers out of defined-benefit plans and into uninsured 401(k) plans. In effect, employees took a hefty pay cut and barely seemed to notice. Proponents of 401(k)s pointed to a changing economy in which employees switch jobs frequently. They maintained that because defined-benefit plans are based on length of service and an average of salaries over the last few years of work, they don't meet the needs of twenty-first century employees. But Congress could have revised the rules and made the plans portable over a working life, just like a 401(k), and retained the guarantee of a fixed retirement amount, just as corporations do for their executives.

As it is, 401(k) portability often impedes efforts to save for retirement. As job-hoppers move from one employer to another, many succumb to the temptation to cash out their 401(k)s and spend the money. Others, when they lose their jobs, are forced to tap into their 401(k)s for money to live on—something they wouldn't be able to do with a pension plan. Studies show that 401(k)s also fail because "workers do not save consistently enough, and when they do, they do not tend to save substantial sums," according to a report by the Center for American Progress.

A total of $3 trillion is in 401(k) accounts. But look beneath that number and you'll see why they are no substitute for pensions. By 2011 the average balance in a 401(k) account was $60,329, according to the Employee Benefit Research Institute (EBRI). But even that modest number does not reveal how inadequate these accounts are for most Americans. Their median value was $17,686—meaning that half the 401(k) accounts held more, and half less. Nearly one in four accounts had a balance of less than $5,000. For most Americans, the amount in their 401(k) account would pay them a retirement benefit of less than $80 a month for life.

But to Wall Street and corporate America, their effort to move millions of Americans out of pensions and into 401(k)-style plans could not have gone better.

In almost every year since 1978, Congress has passed legislation encouraging the shift to 401(k)s, while doing nothing to shore up pension programs. This legislative action doesn't stem from lawmakers' deep-seated philosophical leanings. It has happened because Congress was paid to do so. Changing the rules of the game has been on the to-do list of every major corporate lobbyist for years. The amount of money that just one industry—securities and investment—has invested in Congress over the last two decades tells the story of why the corporate world got its way.

From 1990 to 2012, the financial industry—which includes stockbrokers, investment houses, brokerage firms, and financial planners—contributed $875 million to members of Congress, mainly Republicans, according to the Center for Responsive Politics. And that's not all. From 1998 to 2011, the period for which data are available, the securities and investment industry spent an estimated $900 million lobbying Congress and federal agencies. All that money—at least $2 billion over the last two decades—flowed into Washington from just one industry to buy favors and influence policy.

For the industry, it was money well spent. Corporations saved tens of millions of dollars by eliminating pensions, and the substitution of 401(k)s created a profitable new industry in the financial sector. The proliferation of 401(k)s led to a proliferation of financial planners. Studies show that the administrative costs of 401(k)s are higher than traditional pensions, in part because there is so much overhead as a result of an army of players grasping for a piece of the $3 trillion industry. Even more distressing, the returns of 401(k)s have been, with some exceptions, inferior to those of pensions. Not to mention all the losses suffered during the great crash.

"This is what's wrong with our country," says Robin Gilinger, the United flight attendant who lost nearly two-thirds of her pension. "I think the American public sees it, but they don't know how to stop it. We all see little things. We can see what's going on and how the well-off are manipulating what's happening to us. And there's nothing we can do. So every day you live, hoping to make change, but what change can you make? It's very frustrating."

So it is that, in the end, all but the most affluent senior citizens will have to join the ranks of those like Betty Dizik of Fort Lauderdale, Florida, who is into her seventh decade as a working American. She's had no choice. Betty did not lose her pension. Like most Americans, she never had one, nor did she have a 401(k). After her husband died in 1968, she held a series of jobs managing apartments and self-storage facilities, tasks that brought her into contact with the public. "I like working with people," she said. But none of the jobs offered a pension.

Her monthly Social Security check comes to $1,200. That barely covers her supplemental health insurance, car insurance, and out-of-pocket expenses for medications to treat her heart problems and diabetes. To buy gas for her car and pay rent, utilities, and other living expenses, Betty continued to work long after the age of sixty-five. For years one of her jobs was with Broward County Meals on Wheels, which provides meals to seniors, some younger than she. But by the time she turned seventy-five, driving one hundred miles a day was too much for her, and she gave up the job to work for H&R Block, the tax return service, where she had also worked part-time in varying capacities for years.

She did a little of everything for H&R Block. She was the receptionist and the cashier, the person who opened and closed the office and "took the money to the bank." She worked at H&R Block for nearly twenty years until she was laid off in 2010. By then she was eighty-three. Even so, Betty still needed to work, so she began applying for jobs. When she showed up for interviews, she figured "somebody will hire me because I'm good. I can read. I can write. I can do computers. I am definitely a senior tax preparer, and I am a good manager. I have run offices for many, many years and been complimented on how I run my offices and how my people produce." But in two years she's had only two interviews, and at one she was told, "You're just too old."

A widow, she lives alone in an apartment building for seniors. Her four children pay her rent, but she is reluctant to accept anything more. "All my children are great, but I do not like to ask them for anything," she said.

She doesn't have much hope that Washington will help seniors like her. "They don't understand what it's like to worry: Are you going to be able to make it every month, to pay the telephone bill, the electric bill? How much are you going to have left over for food and other expenses?" Her key to getting by each month is forcing herself to live within a strict budget.

"On the third, I get my Social Security," she said. "On the fourth, I'm broke. I go on and pay all the bills and do what little shopping I have to do, and then I stay home the rest of the month. And I'm not alone. There are a lot just like me."

And thanks to the people who make the rules in America, there will be millions more like her in the future.

CHAPTER 7

DEREGULATION: ECONOMIC CHAOS

It was rare enough for the nation's top banking regulators to be in the same room together with the chiefs of the industry that they regulate, but what captured everyone's attention was the chainsaw.

Standing around a tall stack of *Federal Register*s draped in red tape, the group had assembled on the morning of June 3, 2003, in the offices of the Federal Deposit Insurance Corporation (FDIC) in Washington to declare war on excessive banking regulations, which they claimed were stifling business.

Like those groundbreaking ceremonies where politicians lift a shovel of earth and pose for photos, the banking executives had come prepared for a photo op. Four of them—James McLaughlin of the American Bankers Association, Harry Doherty of America's Community Bankers, Ken Guenther of the Independent Community Bankers of America, and John Reich, the FDIC vice chairman who was the architect of the antiregulation crusade—came sporting long-handled pruning shears. They gathered around the stack of regulations in front of a wall emblazoned every few inches with the words CUTTING RED TAPE in big red letters, and they pretended to trim away at the pile as cameras recorded the scene.

But the undisputed star of the show was the fifth member of the group, James Gilleran, director of the Office of Thrift Supervision (OTS), the federal agency charged with regulating the nation's savings and loan associations. Gilleran was an impassioned foe of government regulations. In his tenure at OTS, he would cut one-quarter of the agency's staff, drastically reducing its oversight ability. To drive home his point on this day, the beaming Gilleran had brought along a chainsaw, and when he jubilantly placed its blade atop the stack of documents, he made it clear to everyone where he stood. "Our goal is to allow thrifts to operate with a wide breadth of freedom from regulatory intrusion" was how he put it later.

Of course, we all know how this worked out. The lack of oversight of companies peddling various kinds of mortgages was a main cause of the financial meltdown in 2008. One of the worst offenders was the OTS, headed until 2005 by Gilleran.

In the annals of bad government agencies, the OTS stands alone. This is the agency that permitted thrifts to peddle home equity loans to homeowners with dementia who could neither understand them nor afford them. It looked the other way when thrifts refused to comply with federal financial laws that were intended to keep them solvent. It allowed lenders to falsify federal reporting documents. It refused to rein in the reckless lending practices that steadily pushed the thrift industry toward a catastrophic fall. It rubber-stamped requests from thrifts, no matter how harebrained, like one from a small bank in the hills of West Virginia to open a branch in upscale Palm Beach Gardens, Florida; ultimately it collapsed. The refusal of the OTS to oversee the industry caused some of the biggest bank failures in U.S. history, including that of Washington Mutual, the largest ever recorded. The agency couldn't even supervise its own officials, one of whom, a regional director, permitted an imperiled thrift, IndyMac, to backdate a capital infusion to make it appear that the company was healthy.

By the end of the George W. Bush era, the OTS was such a monumental disaster that the only solution was to get rid of it and assign its functions to another office in the U.S. Treasury Department. Congress duly merged it with the Office of the Comptroller of the Currency and other divisions. On October 19, 2011, the OTS ceased to exist. But the damage it presided over was not so easy to hide.

The mind-set that brought the banking chiefs together around a chainsaw that morning was a hallmark of the Bush years, when the antigovernment movement long in the making reached full flower. The phrase "get government out of . . ." was everywhere, with the last word filled in according to one's interest: *Get government out of the housing industry. Get government out of health care. Get government out of the economy*. And so on. Government restrictions, we were told, were hamstringing job creation, business development, and entrepreneurship. Regulations concocted in Washington were said to be the biggest obstacle preventing America from achieving its potential. No one stopped to ask the simple but necessary question: Who benefits from the absence of government? Who really enjoys the absence of supervisory regulations?

For the corporate chiefs and other members of the economic elite, having fewer government regulations and laws gives them a freer rein to run the country as they see fit. Their argument goes like this: just leave business and investment alone and everything will work out best. Sure, there are excesses that lead to setbacks; the 2008–2009 recession would qualify. But, deregulators say, such blips are only temporary and the benefits of leaving the economy alone far outweigh the harm done by constraints. Issues such as the minimum wage, the lack of health care for millions, unfair trade competition that kills jobs in the United States— well, those are issues for the market to sort out, not the government. Any intervention in the market by government, the ruling class claims, is destined to fail because it upsets the natural order of things.

For much of the twentieth century in the United States, that view was tempered by the belief that there should be policies that both benefit industry, by establishing a stable and predictable business environment that enables companies to succeed and create jobs, and protect the public interest by helping all classes of Americans to prosper.

From the 1970s onward, the decade when wages, benefits, and so many other economic benefits enjoyed by middle America first began to erode, the deregulators started to gain the upper hand and upset the balance. The wealthy and their supporters founded influential think tanks such as the Heritage Foundation and the Cato Institute. Many more would follow. Ideas propounded by these free-market, antigovernment groups began to receive more credence. Their reports were picked up by the mainstream media, which treated their conclusions as if they were widely shared by the public, although they represented the goals of only a sliver of the populace—the very rich. Funded by corporate chieftains, wealthy Americans, and right-wing ideologues, the think tanks were one of the most important early steps in their plan to remake the country.

As the "no government" ideas of the ruling class gained momentum, basic industries such as airlines and trucking were deregulated, with disastrous results for the industries and the families they once sustained. Nevertheless, deregulators pushed on, with cataclysmic consequences for the housing and mortgage industries, and they continued to lobby for unrestricted free trade to prevent any interference in their ability to ship jobs offshore.

Deregulation is one of the greatest triumphs of America's ruling class, but for middle-class workers and their families the fallout has been devastating:

- The average earnings of airline flight attendants, adjusted for inflation, have declined 31 percent since 1983, based on data from the Bureau of Labor Statistics and the Association of Flight Attendants. Attendants earned $27,160 on average in 1983, according to the association. If their pay had kept pace with inflation, they would earn $61,000. BLS estimated their annual earnings at $41,720 in 2011. That means that since 1983, over nearly two decades, they have lost almost $400,000 in earnings.

- Trucking deregulation, which was enacted to spur economic growth, has caused unprecedented instability in the trucking industry: 43,863 trucking companies have gone out of business since 1990. If truck drivers' annual earnings had kept pace with inflation, they would earn $65,000, adjusted for inflation. Their annual wage in 2011 was $39,830, according to BLS. A trucker working steadily during this time would have lost half a million dollars.

- Abuses in the deregulated financial industry, coupled with other factors, will have caused millions of Americans to lose their homes by 2014.

With isolated exceptions, the economic elite who populate Wall Street, corporate executive suites, and law firms have suffered none of the pain we see in the middle class. Their pay only goes up. A survey by the Institute for Policy Studies (IPS) found that, even after adjusting for inflation, CEOs at fifty companies that laid off the largest number of workers from the beginning of the crash until 2009 walked away with almost $12 million each in 2009.

THE HAVOC BEGINS

The popular perception is that Ronald Reagan was the great deregulator, but airline and trucking deregulation was pushed through Congress by his Democratic predecessor, Jimmy Carter. Many other prominent Democrats who professed concern for working people, including the late senator Edward Kennedy, bought into deregulation and jumped on the bandwagon. It was a mark of how ingeniously the ruling class and like-minded economists and supporters in the media framed the issue: legislation that would unravel the comfortable middle-class lifestyles of hundreds of thousands of Americans was presented as beneficial to the country.

President Carter spoke for politicians from both parties when he signed the airline deregulation bill in 1978: "It will also mean less government interference in the regulation of an increasingly prosperous airline industry."

Backers said the Airline Deregulation Act would stimulate competition, reduce fares, and open up air travel to more Americans. For a brief spell it looked like that might happen. Freed to set fares and schedules, airlines embraced deregulation. New airlines began service, and existing carriers extended routes to new points. Fares went down. Service went up. Competition increased.

It didn't last. In an unregulated market, those with the financial muscle to dominate soon did—the big airlines swallowed the little airlines. New airlines found that they lacked the financial resources to compete. And many long-standing airlines were grounded by excessive competition.

In 2012, there is less competition in the airline industry than before deregulation. In 1978 the ten largest airlines accounted for 88 percent of the revenue from passenger miles flown by U.S. flag carriers. Three decades later, there aren't ten large airlines left in the United States, and the three largest—American, United, and Delta—control two-thirds of domestic air travel. In many markets, airlines have little or no competition, and prices reflect it. In 1977 it cost as little as $86 to fly round-trip from Philadelphia to Pittsburgh; in 2011 the cost was $530—the equivalent of $160 in 1977 dollars.

As predicted, deregulation sparked the birth of many new air carriers, but few survived. The chronic rise and fall of so many airlines has kept the industry in a constant state of upheaval. Since 1978, an estimated 150 low-cost carriers have gone into and *out of* business. New airlines that were once portrayed as deregulation success stories have either collapsed or been absorbed by rivals. In the airline industry, the unregulated free market has been eating its own.

The industry has been hit by wave after wave after wave of bankruptcies since 1978. Pan American, founded in 1927 and the flagship of U.S. carriers, went bankrupt and was liquidated. Eastern Air Lines, also founded in 1926, went bankrupt and was liquidated. Braniff, founded in 1928, filed for bankruptcy three times before it was liquidated. Midway Airlines, founded in 1976, ended up in bankruptcy court and was liquidated. Trans World Airlines, founded in 1925 and one of the nation's most glamorous airlines for decades, went bankrupt and was liquidated. Most of the surviving major airlines—Delta, United, US Airways, Continental, and American—have paid visits to bankruptcy court, some more than once.

Under airline deregulation, bankruptcy costs, operating losses, and other factors have cumulatively drained tens of billions of dollars out of the industry since 1978. Some fares went up, not down. Competition became destructive, not productive. Service was cut back. The increase in air travelers was lower in the decade after deregulation than in the decade before it. Airline travelers overall have fewer choices, and they are often more expensive.

Airline workers have had an even harder time. Since 1978, their wages have gone down, their benefits have been cut, and many have lost their jobs. They must work more hours to earn the same pay. Under pressure from management, work rules have been watered down so that crews for some airlines only have a few hours of rest between international flights—something that wasn't allowed years ago. A study by Demos, a New York think tank, concluded in 2009 that Department of Transportation data showed labor costs falling by one-third on average between 2001 and 2006 for five major airlines—US Airways, United, Delta, American, and Northwest.

For pilots, the cuts have been even deeper. Chesley "Sully" Sullenberger, the heroic US Airways pilot who ferried 155 jet passengers to safety with his remarkable emergency landing in the Hudson River in 2009, saw his pay cut by 40 percent and his pension terminated in the years leading up to his sensational landing. In testimony before Congress in 2009, Sullenberger blamed airline deregulation for placing "pilots and their families in an untenable financial situation."

Robin Gilinger, the United flight attendant we met in Chapter 6, has watched her earnings and those of her coworkers steadily decline over the twenty years she has worked for the airline.

"I'm making less than I made fifteen years ago," she said. "And I'm working more."

For Robin and other airline employees pounded by deregulation, United's bankruptcy filing in 2002 allowed the airline to shred its labor agreements with employees and cut their wages.

"We still are living underneath our bankruptcy wages right now," she said. The only bright spot for her is that because of her seniority she's not worried about losing her job, but the working atmosphere in a once glamorous field has deteriorated markedly.

Despite having negotiated substantial givebacks, employees are constantly pressed by management to give up even more.

Robin said the company is pushing for workers to accept more changes in their work rules that some fear could jeopardize safety. The pressure pits worker against worker, she said, as current employees fight over United's dwindling resources. However it is finally settled, she said, the result will be the same.

"They're making the worker work more to make less."

By nearly every measure, airline deregulation has failed. No one has summed up the adverse consequences better than the longtime head of American Airlines, Robert Crandall, in a 2008 op-ed piece:

> Our airlines, once world leaders, are now laggards in every category, including fleet age, service quality and international reputation. Fewer and fewer flights are on time. Airport congestion has become a staple of late-night comedy shows. An even higher percentage of bags are lost or sent to the wrong airports. Last-minute seats are harder and harder to find. Passenger complaints have skyrocketed. Airline service, by any standard, has become unacceptable.

Nonetheless, the rule-makers hold firm to their contention that deregulation has worked. A paper published by the Cato Institute twenty years after airline deregulation confirmed its unwavering belief in the process: "Despite the criticisms, airline deregulation has provided—and continues to provide—enormous benefits to the average traveler." The Cato paper went on to contend that whatever problems the airline industry had did not stem from "too much reliance on market forces, but from too little."

One of those "market forces" in play will drive down wages even further. The major airlines are rapidly shifting maintenance work on jet aircraft to repair shops offshore. The next time you are on a plane, you might wonder where the aircraft underwent its last major overhaul. Chances are it was at a repair shop in El Salvador, Brazil, or somewhere in Africa. An audit by the inspector general of the U.S. Department of Transportation in 2008 found that 27 percent of heavy airframe maintenance on the largest carriers is outsourced to repair shops outside the United States, many in developing countries. This is the most extensive type of maintenance performed on jets, and it often entails a complete teardown of the aircraft's fuselage over a period of weeks.

The Federal Aviation Administration (FAA) has certified about seven hundred repair shops in seventy countries to work on American jets. Because the FAA's inspections budget is so tight, the agency basically relies on the airlines to police themselves. Even when the FAA does inspect one of these offshore facilities, the plant is alerted ahead of time that inspectors are coming.

Mistakes made in some of these offshore repair shops have caused a few close calls. In January 2009, a US Airways jet flying to Phoenix made an emergency landing in Denver after the pressure seal around the main cabin door began to fail. Authorities later determined that mechanics at a repair shop in El Salvador had installed the seal backward. In another incident, workers at the same El Salvador facility accidentally crossed the wires that connect cockpit gauges to the plane's engines. The mistake was caught by an airline employee before takeoff, avoiding a potential disaster.

Crucial safety work is offshored solely to save money on wages. Airline mechanics in the United States are among the higher-paid blue-collar workers, earning on average $55,000 a year, according to BLS data for 2010. Many earn $100,000 or more. At overhaul bases in Central and South America, mechanics earn only a fraction of that. There are still about 117,000 of these good-paying jobs in the United States, according to the Labor Department in 2011. The department estimates that employment in that sector will be mostly flat in the next few years. But if past outsourcing trends are a guide, and if current policies remain the same, that prediction will turn out to have been wildly optimistic.

In trucking, it's been a similar story. Deregulating the industry was a chief goal of the free-market think tanks and their advocates, who contended that it would make trucking more efficient and produce savings. President Jimmy Carter signed the trucking deregulation bill in July 1980 using words that sounded much like those he had employed two years earlier when he deregulated airlines: "The Motor Carrier Act of 1980 will eliminate the red tape and the senseless overregulation that have hampered the free growth and development of the American trucking industry."

Rather than correct the defects in the regulatory system, Congress threw out the entire system—an overreaction somewhat akin to responding to flawed calls in a football game by eliminating all the referees instead of merely replacing them.

As promised, the law unleashed new competition—on a scale even more destructive than in the airline industry. New trucking companies surged onto the highways by the thousands—and then abruptly ceased to exist. The 43,863 trucking companies that have failed in the last two decades include only companies with five or more trucks. No one has any idea how many smaller trucking companies have come and gone since 1980.

Nearly every large trucking company that was in business at the time of deregulation has either foundered, merged with a competitor, or downsized. Most of those remaining are perilously close to collapse.

The nation's largest trucking company, YRC Freight, is typical. YRC was formed in 2003 by the merger of two of the oldest and most venerable companies in the history of American trucking, Yellow Corporation and Roadway Express, whose roots go back to 1924. Both had struggled for years amid the rapacious price wars set off by deregulation. The merger created a huge company with 36,000 employees and $6 billion in revenue by 2010. But even that didn't work. From 2008 to 2010, YRC lost $1.9 billion. The company avoided bankruptcy court in 2011, at least temporarily, by restructuring its debt and shedding thousands of employees.

The fragile state of the trucking industry has had a dramatic impact on the lives of drivers and their families. Working conditions are more stressful and pay is lower. Like flight attendants, drivers must work more hours to earn the same money. Many are paid according to how many miles they drive, not how long they're on the road. As a result, some have to work as many as eighty to ninety hours a week, living out of the cramped cabs of their trucks and being away from home for weeks at a time. Adding to the stress is the fact that the operating margins for many trucking companies are so narrow that companies cut back on maintenance and replacement of trucks. Truckers' blogs are filled with references to unsafe trucks that are constantly breaking down or posing hazards on the highways.

One of the organizations on the front line of this issue is the Owner-Operator Independent Drivers Association (OOIDA), representing 150,000 independent truckers and drivers on matters from safety to legislation. Sandi Soendker, the editor in chief of *Land Line*, the association's magazine, has seen deregulation up close in her twenty-five years with the association. Throughout that time the industry has been in upheaval, but by 2012 even some old-line trucking companies that managed to survive the cutthroat practices unleashed by deregulation in years past were going under. "We are dealing with this every week," she said.

Soendker said that some companies collapse so suddenly that they leave their drivers stranded:

The companies have been hanging on as long as they can. But when they go under, they'll have drivers out on the road delivering a load. They stop to fuel up, and the fuel card doesn't work. They call the company, but nobody answers.

They are out on the road hung out to dry—with a truck that is not theirs, with a load that is not theirs, and puzzled as to why they can't get through to their dispatcher. What is this guy going to do just to get home? Meanwhile at home, their paycheck has either bounced or never arrived.

She said the chronic instability of the industry has a ripple effect. When a trucking company fails, she said, "everybody gets hurt. Not only the driver behind the wheel but the shipper. How does he get his money?"

Soendker confirmed that even the drivers who have continued to find work have lost ground. "What you get paid for being a truck driver is pitiful," she said. "And it hasn't gotten better for a long time. Everything costs so much more. So if you are making the same amount of money, or just a little bit more, it's costing you five times as much as it did two years ago. Suddenly that little bit of money that you started making is gobbled up by the expenses."

The sword of Damocles for many U.S. truckers is the provision in the North American Free Trade Agreement (NAFTA), the free trade agreement with Mexico, that would allow commercial trucks from Mexico to use U.S. highways. Implementation has been held up for years by legislation, litigation, and safety concerns, but once the remaining litigation is disposed of, Mexican trucks will begin streaming onto U.S. highways.

Many U.S. companies have operations in Mexico that manufacture products for the American market, so one can only imagine the volume of truck traffic that will eventually pour into the States from Mexico. One doesn't need to be a mathematician to understand what will happen. Mexican truck drivers earn about one-third of what U.S. drivers earn.

Even so, the ever-optimistic U.S. Department of Labor says that truck driving is one of the most promising sectors for job growth in coming years.

The deregulation of airlines and trucking has been a catastrophe to the men and women in those industries. It has depressed wages and benefits, engendered chronic job insecurity, and unleashed destructive competition. But because it has saved shippers and consumers a few bucks, that makes it an unqualified success to the deregulators.

UNLEASHING THE BANKS

As successful as they were in remaking those once-stable industries, the real prize for deregulators was money itself: the deregulation of banking.

Proponents included President George H. W. Bush, who predicted in 1991 that banking deregulation would create "a U.S. financial system that protects taxpayers, serves consumers, and strengthens our economy." The reality turned out to be quite different.

Financial deregulation in the United States nearly brought down the global economy in 2008. Wall Street and the banks have since recovered, thanks largely to huge bailouts from tax-payers, such as the Troubled Asset Relief Program (TARP), and capital infusions from the Federal Reserve. But millions of Americans who lost their jobs, their homes, and their retirement savings during the collapse did not receive a bailout and will not recover.

The law that caused a great deal of harm was the Financial Services Modernization Act of 1999, the brainchild of then Texas senator Phil Gramm, the high priest of deregulation in Congress for many years. The law removed regulatory barriers between banks, securities companies, and insurers so that they could sell each other's financial products. In effect, the law let banks become stockbrokers as well as bankers, and it allowed stockbrokers to also become bankers. "I believe that this [law] is the wave of the future," Gramm said upon its passage. After he left the Senate, Gramm became a vice president of UBS, the Swiss banking giant, one of the banks that benefited from the Financial Services Modernization Act. UBS, it should be recalled, later was investigated by the IRS and Justice Department authorities for its role in offshore tax evasion schemes. The bank later agreed to pay $780 million to the United States to settle claims that it had helped cheat the U.S. Treasury out of tax revenue.

The 1999 law repealed parts of the Glass-Steagall Act, which was passed in 1933 to rein in the financial industry excesses that helped cause the Great Depression. Glass-Steagall had worked just fine for decades, but banks hated it because it barred them from selling stocks and mutual funds. Gramm hated it because he said it interfered with the free market. "Government is not the answer," he said after Glass-Steagall was repealed. "We have learned that freedom and competition are the answers. We have learned that we promote economic growth and we promote stability by having competition and freedom."

Along with two laws passed in the early 1980s that would later open the door for exotic mortgages and other lending instruments, the Gramm legislation gave a powerful boost to the deregulation movement in financial services and mortgage lending. The law came along at a time when the mortgage industry was being transformed. Whereas in the past a lender who provided a mortgage held on to the loan and collected interest from the homeowner, now an independent broker arranged the loan, collected a fee, and passed the loan on to someone who bundled it with other mortgages for sale to investors, just as if the mortgages were bonds that guaranteed a solid return.

Before the mortgage industry was deregulated, a lender was careful to make sure the homeowner could repay the loan; otherwise, he'd be stuck with a foreclosed house. But in the new world made possible by Congress, the loan originator didn't care. He got his cut off the top and passed the liability down the line.

What did the mortgage broker care if the loan he'd arranged went bad? He'd already been paid.

This change in the way the business operated opened the door to untold abuses by the financial cowboys and hucksters who gravitated to the field. Fraudulent credit reports, hidden interest charges, usurious loan rates—all of these were by-products of the gold rush to generate more and more loans. The more loans, the more fees. This frenetic activity helped power an entirely new market in so-called subprime mortgages—loans to homeowners with below-par credit or few assets were charged higher rates of interest for their loans, which then generated much larger fees for the lenders. By the time Gramm's bill was passed, the subprime market had grown to $150 billion—a 600 percent increase in just five years. In the next decade, it would grow ten times more.

So in 1999, at a time when the industry needed more oversight than ever by federal regulators, the message out of Congress couldn't have been clearer: allow Wall Street, banks, the financiers, and everyone else connected with this go-go industry to continue conducting their business without any interference.

Legal aid lawyers and consumer groups saw clearly what was happening and warned Congress that the run-up in subprime lending and other abuses in the mortgage field were paving the way for an impending collapse, but the industry poured millions of dollars into campaign contributions to lawmakers to deflect opposition. Among the recipients of the industry's largesse was

Bob Ney, a Republican congressman from Ohio, who was chairman of the House Financial Services Committee's housing subcommittee. Ney, a figure in the Jack Abramoff lobbying scandal, later went to jail after pleading guilty to charges of conspiring to defraud the federal government and falsifying financial disclosure forms.

The lenders, in the best Washington tradition, created a lobbying committee with a friendly-sounding name—Coalition for Fair and Affordable Lending. It had little to do with fairness, but a lot to do with bad loans. Its membership was loaded with subprime loan companies, and they had just the right lobbyist: Wright Andrews Jr., a former senatorial aide who, as one commentator later put it, had "developed a niche representing some of the least sympathetic and most predatory players in the financial industry." From 2003 through 2007, the Coalition spent $6.7 million lobbying, with $3.2 million going to Andrews's law firm.

Every attempt by consumer groups and lawyers for mortgage victims to amend the law and impose more stringent regulations on lenders failed.

The rest is history. Since 2007, an estimated 12 million home foreclosures have been filed; at least 4 million Americans have lost their homes, and millions more are in danger of losing theirs; the average price for existing homes in the United States has dropped more than 20 percent, and more than $5 trillion in home equity has vaporized.

WRECKING LIVES

It is possible to see how financial deregulation is playing out up close in the real world in a one-story stucco building just off busy Del Prado Boulevard in Cape Coral, Florida. Tucked into the center of a row of storefronts is the headquarters of the Invest in America's Veterans Foundation of Cape Coral. Started in 2009, it was sparked by the work of a group of veterans organized by Ralph Santillo, a veteran from New Jersey who relocated to Cape Coral decades ago. A home builder, Santillo had been driven out of business by the collapse of Florida real estate. While fighting his own financial demons, he kept running into other veterans who were also increasingly desperate. They had lost jobs as well as their savings and feared they were about to lose their homes. "The stories were heartbreaking," he said.

Together with other veterans, including Donald Graf, a retired advertising man from New York, they formed the foundation as a service agency for veterans in southwest Florida. In the beginning, Santillo operated out of his home or the trunk of his car until grants from local businesses enabled the foundation to lease the office on Del Prado. Since then, the place has quickly become a magnet for troubled veterans in Cape Coral and the surrounding area.

On any given day, the office is buzzing as veterans come in seeking counseling and volunteers answer a steady stream of phone calls from other former service personnel in need. A disproportionate number of former military personnel—an estimated 60,000—have settled in the area. It has two attractions: a climate beneficial to those with service-related ailments and affordability.

Santillo said the foundation soon found that it has to deal with a whole catalog of ills—veterans who can't navigate Veterans Administration (VA) procedures to claim benefits, others who don't even know they are entitled to VA assistance, and still others who are desperate to find work. The lack of jobs is especially traumatic for younger veterans, many of whom served multiple tours in Iraq or Afghanistan only to return home and find there's no work for them.

"This is a lost generation for jobs," said Graf. "These kids are not being hired, and everything politically is being done to stop that because some states are using expanded child labor laws to use teenagers without having to compensate them for their work. And they want seniors to work longer. So all the jobs veterans would get are not there for them."

As grim as things are for young veterans, foundation volunteers realized that some older veterans were in even more trouble. With service dating as far back as the Korean War, some veterans were on the verge of losing their houses. They became victims of predatory mortgage practices—a by-product of deregulation. Santillo recalled that most of those who refinanced or took out home equity loans were just trying to get money to survive.

"They're living on a fixed income, usually just Social Security, sometimes a little pension," he said. "All their costs are going up—insurance, taxes. Most times when people refinanced they used that money just to keep up with their bills and pay their mortgage. So there was no real benefit. It was not like people were going to get rich and live off the money."

Many didn't realize the potential ramifications of the loans they were assuming. "There was stuff out there like no-interest loans or loans where you paid 1 percent interest," Santillo said. "Then all of a sudden you find out two years down the road you are paying $5,000 a month. Some of these were usurious. They would have put you in jail for that years ago."

But thanks to deregulation, nobody went to jail. Nobody broke any rules because that's what deregulation means: there are no rules to break. Instead, mortgage brokers and banks were rewarded with lucrative fees in the new mortgage industry that was playing out in Cape Coral and a thousand other places like it across America.

In Florida the process was exacerbated when thousands of ex-cons looking for a way to make a quick buck surged into the Florida mortgage industry and began writing mortgages. A *Miami Herald* investigation in 2009 found that 10,529 persons with criminal records worked in Florida's mortgage industry from 2000 to 2007. Of those brokers, 4,065 had committed major crimes—fraud, bank robbery, racketeering, or extortion.

Despite widespread evidence that the foreclosure crisis was in part a result of runaway greed by an out-of-control, unregulated industry, Congress and Washington pundits have since contended that the crisis was caused by the federal government's overzealous attempt to promote homeownership. Under this theory, by easing up on the rules for granting mortgages, the government allowed people who didn't really have the income or assets to buy their first homes. It's a convenient way to shift the blame away from Washington and Wall Street, which caused the calamity to the victims who paid the price.

Most of the victims facing foreclosure who have talked with Santillo, Graf, and other foundation volunteers in Cape Coral are not first-time homeowners. Many had owned homes for years, but found themselves in financial trouble after unscrupulous salesmen signed them up for exotic mortgages with hidden interest clauses that were ticking time bombs. When the interest rate shot up, many lost their home.

John Aguiar is a veteran of the Gulf War, a former intelligence analyst for the Army who took part in Operation Desert Storm in 1990. After graduating from high school in Chicago, he trained at the U.S. Army's legendary intelligence training post at Fort Huachuca, the secretive enclave in remote southern Arizona, where he learned the intricacies of signal intelligence and mapping. After Saddam Hussein invaded Kuwait, John was deployed to Iraq to provide reconnaissance for the infantry.

When his tour of duty ended, he returned to Chicago and married Syrena, his high school sweetheart. They bought a house in suburban Chicago, where their daughter and son were born. In 2002, with John concerned that his job might not be secure, they moved to Cape Coral, where Syrena's parents lived. John was a midlevel manager in the trucking industry, a field that had become chronically unstable after Congress deregulated the industry in 1980. Only months after he and his family moved to Florida, his former employer—Consolidated Freightways, one of the nation's oldest long-haul truckers—filed for bankruptcy and went out of business.

In Cape Coral the Aguiars bought a lot and built a house that reflected their values and their way of life. It was nothing fancy: a one-story Cape rancher with three bedrooms, two baths, and a two-car garage. There were no granite countertops, no Jacuzzi—just the basics, in keeping with what they could afford. "We didn't do lavish things," said Syrena, "but we sank everything into the place. This was the home we had always wanted." It was where they planned to raise their kids and retire. To support the family, John landed a job with a building materials company.

Their troubles began when the city of Cape Coral hit them with an unexpected bill for $20,000 to connect to the city's water and sewer system. When they built their house, they had been led to believe that city water and sewer were years away, so they had spent $22,000 to drill a well and build a septic system. To come up with $20,000 more, they were forced to refinance.

Their original mortgage was a 6 percent fixed-rate loan, but this time the mortgage company substituted an adjustable rate. "I didn't know it was an adjustable-rate mortgage until it was a done deal," said Syrena. "Then it was too late." At first they were able to handle the new monthly payment, which rose from $1,100 a month to $1,400.

But the interest rate on the new mortgage continued to climb just as the Florida economy began to falter. Worried that his job in a housing-related field might not be safe, John began moonlighting twenty to twenty-five hours a week on nights and weekends at a Home Depot. Then his company closed its office in his area and he lost his day job.

John and Syrena scraped to pay the mortgage, cutting back on expenses and depleting their savings and retirement accounts. Their monthly mortgage payment soared to $2,000. "The mortgage payment just kept getting higher," said John, "and we kept sending out one more payment, one more payment, one more payment, until we could figure out what we were going to do." They tried to negotiate with their mortgage company to lower the interest rate, "but they didn't want anything to do with us," said Syrena.

The Aguiars were swept aside by one of the powerful forces driving foreclosures: the company servicing the mortgage did not own the loan and thus had no incentive to offer the family an arrangement that might let them stay in their home until they got back on their feet financially. In 2009, with their mortgage company turning a deaf ear, the Aguiars could no longer come up with the ever-higher monthly mortgage payments and were facing foreclosure. Just before they were to appear in foreclosure court, the mortgage company gave them permission to short-sell their house. It sold fairly quickly—at a loss—and the family moved in with Syrena's parents.

Unable to find work in Florida, John took a job in shipping with a trucking company in Chicago. Syrena and their daughter and son remained in Florida, where the children attended schools that both parents said provided them an excellent education. Meghan, fourteen, hoped to become a veterinarian; eleven-year-old Jacob's goal was to be a robotic engineer. John couldn't visit them for nearly a year after he took the Chicago job, in part because of unexpected medical problems that included a hospital stay for complications from diabetes. So when the family wanted to get together, it usually had to be by phone.

When they had their house in Cape Coral, Syrena recalled, she and John felt like they had everything:

"We had our family. We had good jobs, we had a nice house that we built, we had a dog, we had a cat, and we were happy. And then one day we woke up and everything started going backward on us. We just want to get our lives back together."

In an earlier time, things would have been different. After World War II and the Korean War, the federal government oversaw housing programs that did not permit the kinds of financial gimmickry by Wall Street, banks, and investors that have proven so destructive to the Aguiars, other veterans, and millions of other middle-class Americans.

"We had the American dream," said Syrena, "and it was taken from us."

CHAPTER 8

GLOBALIZATION SHANGHAIED

American politicians are always talking about creating jobs. So why is it they are always killing jobs?

A look at two industries reveals a pattern. Rose growing and circuit board manufacture could hardly seem more different, but what happened to them was the same. How it happened and why it happened is a story often repeated in America, and the tale almost always ends badly.

A generation ago, greenhouses that grew long-stemmed roses flourished in American communities from coast to coast, supplying florists with abundant homegrown bouquets on Valentine's Day, Mother's Day, and other special occasions. Many greenhouses had been owned by the same families for generations, and some towns, like Madison, New Jersey, which called itself "The Rose City," proudly defined themselves by the industry.

Today almost all the greenhouses are gone. More than 90 percent of the roses sold in America are imported, mostly from Colombia. They are grown on the high plateau near Bogota and harvested by peasants, then loaded into jumbo jets for flights to Miami. The most common explanation as to why this happened is that American growers couldn't compete because of cheap labor and ideal growing conditions in the Andes. Those were certainly factors, but there's a more important reason. The U.S. government helped drive the American rose industry out of business.

Starting in the 1960s, the U.S. Agency for International Development (USAID), the arm of the State Department that encourages economic growth in poor nations, gave Colombia financial assistance to spur the growth of its flower-export industry. U.S.-funded technicians helped Colombian growers cultivate their crops and create a distribution network to get their flowers to market. In so doing, U.S. taxpayers helped pay the start-up costs for an industry that eventually would destroy one of America's own.

Once Colombia's flower industry was firmly established, producing ever-greater quantities for export, the federal government, no doubt at the urging of the State Department, allowed the flowers to be imported into the United States without facing high tariffs. Colombia's first flower exports, carnations, quickly overwhelmed American carnation growers. Roses, a much more lucrative crop, came next.

As rose imports quickly cut into the domestic industry, rose growers turned to the U.S. government for help, starting in the

1980s. They didn't get it. Almost every time they lodged a complaint with U.S. trade authorities concerning unfair trading practices, government officials sided with Colombian growers and against U.S. companies.

This has been the pattern for years in scores of U.S. industries: domestic producers plead for help only to encounter indifference and denial about what is happening to their companies. In response to an impassioned plea from domestic rose growers in 1984, the U.S. International Trade Commission issued this adamant refusal to intervene:

> Imports of fresh-cut roses from Colombia have had no material impact on the domestic industry. . . . The domestic industry is in a healthy condition; domestic production, shipments, profits and productivity have all increased. . . .
>
> Potential increases in imports from Colombia present no threat of material injury to the domestic industry because the industry has exhibited the strength to withstand import competition, and the projected increase in imports is small relative to the domestic market and past increases.

Were U.S. trade officials blind to what was happening, or were they just in the grip of special interests? In the end it made no difference to the American rose growers. The assertion that the U.S. industry was healthy was just plain wrong. The rose industry was already dying, due to Washington. When the trade commission claimed all was well, rising imports accounted for 22 percent of domestic consumption. By the end of 2011, imports had taken over all but 10 percent of the market.

Workers in old industries such as roses are often urged to learn a new trade so they can compete in the new economy. Woe to any of them who studied how to make printed circuit boards. From personal computers to cell phones, circuit boards are the heart and soul of all electronic devices. The internal plates to which chips and other components are attached, circuit boards connect the various parts of a device to make it work.

The circuit board industry developed in the United States and has been at the center of high-tech innovation. From a lone plant that opened in 1952 outside Chicago, circuit boards had become a $10 billion U.S. industry by 2000, one that produced 30 percent of the world's supply. With that amount of business, the United States had all kinds of potential economies of scale to support the industry. To little avail.

With high technology constantly cited as pivotal to America's economic future, one might have expected that this crucial cog in the high-tech machine would get an assist from Washington; after all, helping this industry would benefit not only industry workers but the nation as a whole. But Washington had other ideas. In the grip of free-trade ideas that would brook no actions that might be considered protectionist, Washington impassively stood by as foreign producers in China and South Korea, among others, subsidized and supported by their governments, undercut domestic producers.

Over the years, domestic manufacturers appealed to Congress for help, citing the unfair trade practices that were destroying them. Congress turned a deaf ear. By 2012, the U.S. industry had only a few hundred circuit board makers, and the nation's output has shrunk to around $3 billion a year, less than one-third of what it was just a decade earlier.

The first plant that made circuit boards in the United States, Bartlett Manufacturing in Cary, Illinois, shut down in 2009, after fifty-seven years in business. Douglas Bartlett, whose father founded the company, said he could no longer compete against the predatory trade policies orchestrated by the Chinese government. With the loss of this domestic industry, the United States is forfeiting its high-tech future.

"Our kids are going to be fluffing dogs and doing toenails while the Chinese are making leading-edge devices," Bartlett told *Manufacturing & Technology News,* a sophisticated Washington, D.C., newsletter that tracks globalization, foreign trade, and other issues affecting American manufacturers.

The Chinese were eclipsing the United States in more than just high technology. On a summer day in 2010, Arnold Schwarzenegger, then governor of California, paid a visit to a factory to thank an enthusiastic crowd of steelworkers for their hard work in casting the steel for one of America's iconic bridges—the new Bay Bridge linking San Francisco and Oakland.

"There was one thing that I demanded from my staff, and that was that . . . I can go and visit the workers that are building our Bay Bridge, so that I have a chance to say 'thank you, thank you, thank you for the great work you are doing,'" he told the assembled workers. "You have done an extraordinary job because so many of you go to work every day and do welding, painting, lifting, designing, shipping, all of those things in order to help us in California rebuild our Bay Bridge."

The steelworkers erupted in applause and rushed to shake Schwarzenegger's hand or stand next to him, a typical crowd reaction to the Hollywood movie star turned politician. It was the kind of scene that has played out countless times in America down through the years when politicians pay homage to those who actually build our monuments, from the Empire State Building to the Golden Gate Bridge.

But this time the setting wasn't Pittsburgh, Chicago, or Los Angeles. Schwarzenegger was standing in a steel plant thirty minutes outside Shanghai. Zhenhua Heavy Industries had won the multibillion-dollar contract to cast the steel components that make up the eight-mile-long span across San Francisco Bay.

How did a landmark bridge project in America—one that presented a serious engineering challenge, the kind that was once the staple of American manufacturing—end up in the mills of Shanghai?

The story starts in 1989, the year the original bridge was severely damaged in the Loma Prieta earthquake centered south of San Francisco. The quake killed sixty-three people, including a motorist on the bridge when one section of the roadway collapsed. The bridge, which is often the nation's busiest toll bridge—it carries nearly 300,000 vehicles a day—was described as "unstable" and had to be closed for a month for repairs.

Years of wrangling over the design and financing of the replacement bridge followed, but eventually local and state politicians agreed on a design for an innovative, self-anchored suspension bridge with a tower rising to the height of a fifty-two-story building. That's the part of the bridge that will be memorialized by a "Made in China" label.

From the start, there was a decidedly pro-China tilt to the process of bidding for the project. Schwarzenegger had urged the Chinese to submit a bid. Ultimately the project went to a joint venture between the Chinese and the American Bridge Company of Coraopolis, Pennsylvania, a legendary name among American bridge builders. Steel from American Bridge had gone into San Francisco's Golden Gate Bridge and New York's Brooklyn Bridge as well as some of the nation's most famous office towers, including the Woolworth and Chrysler Buildings in Manhattan. But this time the steel was to be cast in China; American Bridge no longer made steel. It was just an assembler.

Even the president and chief executive officer of American Bridge, Robert H. Luffy, favored China, believing that Chinese steel would be cheaper than American. He also didn't believe that any U.S. companies were capable of handling such a big job. As he explained to a congressional subcommittee during a 2007 hearing:

> The largest steel fabricating facility in the United States for bridges . . . is probably 300 or 400 people on the floor working. I was in a facility that is going to fabricate the steel for the Oakland Bay Bridge. . . . They have 32,000 people in that facility. It is not even a contest. It is not even a contest.

The United States was not the steel power it once had been. Years of allowing low-cost imports subsidized by foreign governments had decimated American steelmaking. A succession of U.S. Congresses and administrations from both parties occasionally complained about unfair trade practices, but the complaints always made little headway, as neither Democrats nor Republicans had the backbone to do anything substantive about them for fear of antagonizing our trading partners. Consequently, the once-powerful steel industry slowly shriveled.

But that didn't mean the United States was incapable of producing steel for the Bay Bridge. Even though there was no longer one company, such as Bethlehem Steel, that could do the work, the job could have been done by a consortium. And such a consortium could have been created if there had been the slightest encouragement and assistance from policymakers in California and Washington.

Oregon Iron Works in Clackamas, Oregon, was ready to be part of a consortium. Tom Hickman, the company's vice president, said a group of Oregon steel fabricators was ready to build a new plant to manufacture girders for the Bay Bridge. "We put together a group that was willing to put up $30 million to build a new facility on the Columbia River," he said. In what could have been "really a countrywide effort," Hickman said, "other parts of the project could have gone to steel mills in Illinois, Indiana, and Pennsylvania." The contract, he said, could have provided jobs for fabricators, plate makers, drivers, material handlers, and others. "The chain of events goes out everywhere and probably would have affected almost every state," he said.

Because of its size and unique design, the new Bay Bridge was a daunting engineering and manufacturing challenge. But the sheer daring and unknowns involved in such a revolutionary design were considerations that the American bidders may have factored into their original bid but that their Chinese opponents overlooked or ignored.

Nevertheless, the contract went to the Chinese. The California Department of Transportation (Caltrans) bought into the argument that it was easier and cheaper to go with the Chinese. The cheaper argument, which would later turn out to have been a fallacy, always plays well with American politicians and bureaucrats in the beginning, even if it often doesn't work out that way in the end. They count on the short-term memory loss of the country's voters. Any serious idea that the work might be done in the

United States was never entertained. The Bay Bridge project exemplifies how some politicians have abandoned even the pretense that they want to create jobs in America.

After the contract was awarded, problems surfaced in the quality of the work being done in China. Initial checks found that as many as 65 percent of the welds failed to meet specifications. To oversee the work, Caltrans had to dispatch two hundred engineers and contractors to China to provide technical advice, answer questions, and make sure the finished pieces met specifications. The Caltrans engineers were in China for months, their work there adding significantly to the original cost.

Schwarzenegger had justified awarding the contract to China on the basis of numerous savings he claimed it would produce. By his count, he saved $400 million for his state when the contract went to Shanghai. His calculation did not, however, take into account the wages lost by steelworkers and ironworkers who otherwise would have been employed on the project and which could have run into the hundreds of millions of dollars. It did not take into account the taxes those workers would have paid, from state income taxes to Social Security and unemployment taxes, a figure that would easily have totaled tens of millions of dollars. It did not take into account the multiplier effect of potentially hundreds of millions of dollars as well from all the potential benefits derived from the daily purchases made by people with jobs. It did not take into account all the local taxes that employed workers pay for schools and local government. Nor did it take into account all the tax revenue that state and local governments had to expend for unemployment, health care, and other costs run up by people who have no jobs. All told, hundreds of millions of dollars would have stayed in the United States and been plowed back into our economy. In short, what might look like a "savings" was anything but. The ultimate cost of the bridge is anyone's guess, although some estimates put the figure for the entire project, including interest, at $12 billion. What's clear is that the United States lost an exceptional opportunity to create good-paying jobs at home during a time of high domestic unemployment.

"If that investment could have been made here, it could have provided jobs here," said Oregon Iron's Hickman. "These jobs are living-wage jobs and family-wage jobs. They provide health and welfare benefits, 401(k)s, and pensions. Our facilities meet all of the environmental requirements, and it just is a very, very difficult thing to compete with the Chinese when you are really competing with the Chinese government." Or when Oregon Iron and other domestic producers find themselves competing against not only the Chinese government but their own government.

The contrast between the actions of today's policymakers and those who built the original Bay Bridge is dramatic. Construction started and ended during the Great Depression, providing urgently needed jobs, with financing arranged by a new government entity created to boost employment, the Reconstruction Finance Corporation (RFC). The steel for the bridge was the largest order ever placed for steel in the United States up to that time, and it put thousands of steelworkers and suppliers to work for years, generating income for their families and their communities. One of the largest infrastructure investments ever made up to then, the bridge once completed returned many times its original cost over the years in its boost to commerce and industry in the Bay Area alone.

By creating jobs for Chinese steelworkers, American politicians are making it all but certain that the domestic steel industry will continue to weaken. If it is an industry in which no one company today is capable of doing work on the scale of the Bay Bridge, then after another Bay Bridge or two, not even multiple U.S. companies will be able to tackle such undertakings, and the blue-collar workers will be followed out the door by the white-collar professionals—the engineers and draftsmen.

That's what makes Schwarzenegger's words in a factory in Shanghai all the more poignant. Any number of American workers would have loved the chance to weld, paint, lift, design, ship, and perform all the other chores required to help California rebuild its Bay Bridge. But they were not given that opportunity. Nor is it likely that they will be offered a stake in any similar undertaking in the future. U.S. politicians in thrall to a simplistic trade ideology would rather create jobs for people in China than for American workers.

JUSTIFYING JOB LOSSES

The chief culprit in the destruction of good jobs in America is this country's blind adherence to unrestricted free trade.

The concept of free trade goes back to the writings of Adam Smith and David Ricardo in the eighteenth and nineteenth centuries; these theorists held that trading nations should do away with tariffs and freely accept each other's products. As the theory goes, the country that can make a product most cheaply should specialize in that item and sell it to other countries, which enables that country to earn the money to buy specialized goods from other countries. In this ideal global economy, everybody is open to each other's products, and whoever has the best or cheapest wins out in this level playing field. It's a simple theory, and there is much to recommend it—providing that all trading nations abide by the same rules.

But the simple theory bears scant resemblance to the version of free trade practiced in this country. Here there is little or no attempt to promote fair trade. There are no safeguards for domestic workers and industries. There's no attempt to balance exports and imports, hence our mammoth trade deficit. U.S. trade policy has essentially been hijacked by multinational corporations, which have found it in their interest to ship work abroad and then bring products made offshore back to the United States while paying the lowest possible tariffs. This wide-open policy has enriched the biggest corporations, but it has been catastrophic for many U.S. industries at home and for millions of workers.

While the United States has lowered its trade barriers and now welcomes imports from around the world, many of our trading partners are not as open and commonly erect trade barriers to

U.S. products. Japan has consistently frustrated efforts by the American auto industry to export products to Japan. When American businesses and workers protest these unfair trade practices and call for tariffs or some other penalty against an offending country to level the playing field, free-traders such as the Cato Institute or the Heritage Foundation in the United States go ballistic and claim that tariffs would violate principles of free trade and would be a form of protectionism. Their oft-heard charge is, "We can't build walls around the country." To levy tariffs against a nation that has failed to live up to basic trading rules is not protectionist: it's called equity for American workers and businesses.

To make matters worse, many nations subsidize industries that make products specifically designed for export to America. Produced at an artificially low cost, these goods sell for less than the same products made in the United States. That kills jobs and businesses here, and it's a basic violation of free trade: nations aren't supposed to bankroll their companies to gain an export advantage. But many do, and they are rarely forcefully challenged by the United States.

The Chinese are masters of the art. China's government subsidizes numerous enterprises that compete directly with American businesses. Moreover, the Chinese government has weak labor and environmental laws and regulations. For many U.S. companies, it is remarkable that they can compete at all, given the way the deck is stacked against them.

The fathers of free trade—Smith and Ricardo—never envisioned a world in which developing nations would be sending their products to developed nations. Their concept of free trade depended on two conditions: first, that the countries trading would have fundamentally shared value systems; and second, that because of the time involved in the transportation of goods by sail (they had not envisaged the trading of services exactly), local products would always retain a competitive edge. Neither factor applies anymore. Smith and Ricardo never envisioned a time when a domestic manufacturer would invest in a foreign plant to produce products for the home market. Smith, whose *Theory of Moral Sentiments* was as important to him as the *Wealth of Nations,* which is selectively cited by free-trade ideologues, would have decried a financial relationship that based short-term profit on the ability to outsource manufacture to countries whose labor conditions were worse in every way. In Smith and Ricardo's model, countries with similar economies would open their markets to one another to exchange locally produced goods and reciprocal courtesies in the same way that the present-day European Union operates.

No matter what free-traders in the United States say about the wonders of open markets, the Chinese are pursuing an entirely different approach as they target one industry after another through aggressive trade policies. Solar power was briefly viewed as one of America's most promising new industries. Solar photovoltaics, the alternative energy technology on which the greatest hopes are pinned, was invented in the United States at Bell Laboratories in 1954. By the 1980s, the United States was the leading manufacturer of solar photovoltaic panels to generate electricity for businesses and homeowners. Yet by 2011, the Chinese had taken over the market: by then, more than 50 percent of the solar photovoltaic panels installed in America were made by Chinese companies. Chinese solar imports jumped from $21.3 million in 2005 to $2.65 *billion* in 2011.

What happened?

In the last decade, the Chinese government set out to capture the market for manufacturing solar panels. It pumped the equivalent of billions of dollars into the country's nascent solar industry in low-cost loans, subsidies to buy land, discounts for water and power, tax exemptions, and export grants. Government aid to subsidize an export industry is illegal under global trading rules, but the Chinese forged ahead and soon cornered the world market on solar photovoltaic panels. China's exports of solar cells and panels to the United States rose a phenomenal 350 percent in just three years, from 2008 to 2010.

As massive volumes of Chinese government–supported solar cells and panels surged into the United States, prices in the domestic market collapsed. The Coalition for American Solar Manufacturing, in an October 2011 trade action, explained the consequences:

> The resulting price collapse has had a devastating impact on the U.S. solar cell and panel industry, resulting in shut-

downs, layoffs, and bankruptcies throughout the country. Over the past 18 months, seven solar plants have shut down or downsized, eliminating thousands of U.S. solar manufacturing jobs in Arizona, California, Massachusetts, Maryland, New York, and Pennsylvania.

One of those plants, in Frederick, Maryland, had grown steadily since opening in 1982 and for a long time had been thought to have a promising future. Owned by BP Solar, the plant had undergone a major expansion as recently as 2006 so it could produce more collectors for the burgeoning U.S. market. But in October 2010, BP suddenly closed the plant, throwing more than three hundred machine operators out of work. The company couldn't match the cutthroat pricing of the Chinese.

In March 2012, responding to a complaint by the U.S. solar manufacturing industry, the U.S. Commerce Department ruled that China did indeed engage in unfair trade practices in the solar industry, but the additional tariffs the Obama administration imposed on Chinese solar products were so low—ranging from 2.90 to 4.73 percent—as to be meaningless. Even if stiffer tariffs are assessed, the U.S. solar manufacturing industry has been so weakened by Chinese trade practices that it has little hope of regaining its position as a major player.

Despite the obvious damage that unrestricted free trade is causing in the lives of many American workers, the policy remains firmly in place. The economic elite wouldn't have it any other way. They view free trade as a way to hold down wages and increase profits—which lead to higher dividends and more robust stock prices. In the corporate world, America's multinationals are the most ardent backers of unrestricted free trade. And why not? Free trade lets them operate much more freely than if they were bound only by the laws and labor market of the United States. Free trade allows them to pursue a bottom-line strategy without concern for the social consequences, in the United States or elsewhere.

The politicians, in hock to the corporate elite and other members of the ruling class, have fallen into line on free trade. They routinely enact legislation that U.S. multinational corporations request to "liberalize" trade laws. They mouth the same platitudes of corporate America about the evils of protectionism and the wonders of free markets. They dismiss any concerns about what such laws will do to the domestic labor market, urging workers to go back to school so they can compete in the new economy.

In addition to politicians, financial types, corporate executives, and economists, free trade has one other influential group of supporters. This is the media. Generally speaking, when a trade dispute arises, the media invariably come down on the side of unrestricted free trade and portray those who question its merits as protectionists or reactionaries out of touch with modern times.

Prominent among these advocates is Thomas Friedman, the *New York Times* columnist who set forth his views extensively in his best-selling book *The World Is Flat.* After weighing the pros and cons of free trade, Friedman wrote:

Even as the world gets flat, America as a whole will benefit more by sticking to the general principles of free trade, as it always has, than by trying to erect walls, which will only provoke others to do the same and impoverish us all.

Like all free-trade boosters, Friedman speaks in absolutes: either you have free trade or you are a protectionist; either you leave the door wide open to imports or you build a wall around the country. The idea that a nation might selectively apply tariffs or other sanctions when a domestic industry is unfairly targeted isn't discussed as a possibility. But that is precisely how such a policy could be applied. In truth, the United States has never come close to erecting a picket fence on the border, let alone a wall.

Friedman contends, as do other free-traders, that all nations benefit from free trade, and he cites trade between India and the United States as an example. By allowing the free flow of commerce between the two nations, Friedman says, each nation has benefited, and "one can see evidence of this mutual benefit in the sharp increase in exports and imports between the United States and India in recent years." That imports and exports between the two nations rose is correct. But the biggest increase was in the U.S. trade deficit with India. From 2000 to 2011, it more than doubled, from $7 billion in 2000 to $14.5 billion in 2011—an all-time high. Like most of our major trading partners, India sells more to us than it buys from us—a trade gap that widens every year.

Friedman does recognize that free trade causes displacements, and as a solution he offers two ideas that have long been part of the free-trade manifesto. The first, as we discussed earlier, is to educate working Americans to give them the skills that will enable them to compete in the global economy. This should be accompanied, Friedman contends, by "a foreign strategy of opening restricted markets all over the world . . . thereby bringing more countries into the global free-trade system."

For decades the United States has negotiated agreements to open foreign markets. In Japan's case alone, the United States has followed this route countless times, cutting deals that supposedly would allow our products into the Japanese market. But there has been very little penetration. Most U.S. products and services still haven't made headway in Japan. When a trade agreement isn't honored, as has long been the case with Japan, how can the United States enforce the law other than by building, at least temporarily, a wall to keep out certain Japanese products? But Friedman and other free-traders are against walls of any kind. So we are left with unenforceable agreements that are selectively ignored to suit their own domestic needs by our so-called trading "partners." This casual disregard for the way export markets are rigged against U.S. business has to cease. Otherwise, we have to ask: free trade is free for whom exactly? It's costing us plenty.

Free-trade advocates say that American consumers are the beneficiaries of U.S. trade policy. But the real winners are America's multinational corporations. Free trade has given them enormous power and influence—the ability to depress the wages of U.S. workers, to move jobs at will around the globe, to richly reward executives, and to pay handsome dividends to stockholders.

Thanks to Washington's rule makers, a global corporation that moves its operations to a cheap labor zone anywhere in the world can bring its product back into the United States with few if any import duties and sell it in the domestic market for the same price it charged when the product was made by workers in Dubuque, Iowa. Congress has sweetened the deal even further with tax policies that allow corporations to park billions of earnings in offshore accounts beyond the reach of the U.S. Treasury—tax-free.

It's natural for corporations to pursue their self-interest, but in decades past, Washington set policies that struck a balance between those interests and those of the nation as a whole. The complete triumph of free-trade ideology has upset that balance. For many Americans, this has meant stagnant or declining earnings, reduced benefits, and fewer job opportunities. This is not the result of inexorable global economic forces. These trade and tax policies were bought and paid for by the major corporations through their investments in congressmen and the lobbyists who know their way around Washington.

Although workers have paid the steepest price for free trade, costs have also been heavy for thousands of domestic companies— like Bartlett Manufacturing—that were unable or unwilling to move their operations offshore. For them, free trade has been a disaster. And those that survive often pay taxes at a higher rate than the multinational corporations that have relocated offshore.

Even when an effort is made in Washington to try to help domestic industries fighting for their lives against unfair trade practices, the money on the other side overwhelms it. In 2008 U.S. Customs and Border Protection proposed a change in the way duties are assessed on imported goods. Customs had long suspected that multinational corporations and importers were not declaring the full cost of goods they produced overseas. This deprived Treasury of revenue and made the cost of the imported goods artificially low, which undercut domestic manufacturers and their workers.

Customs proposed using a system that would conform with the way most other nations value imports. Even China, where most of the U.S. imports were made, uses a system similar to the one proposed by Customs. The change was supported by a trade association, the American Manufacturing Trade Action Coalition (AMTAC), composed of about one hundred domestic manufacturers, many in the textile industry.

But to the trade lobby, the change meant war. To scuttle the proposal, Boeing, Xerox, and other multinational interests joined forces with other importing companies as well as lobbyists for several foreign governments. Under the direction of their Washington lobbyist, himself a former customs official, they formed an ad hoc committee called the First Sale Coalition—so named for an obscure provision in customs law by which imported items are valued for tariff purposes. A friendly congressman then inserted a clause on their behalf in a pending bill to put the Customs proposal on hold. Eventually, they succeeded in killing it altogether. The ruling class had showed once more how firmly it was in control of the system.

***

FOR YEARS AMERICAN policymakers have tried to fool the electorate into believing that in a global economy everything will eventually work out. Poor countries with lots of cheap labor will take the dirty, unskilled jobs, leaving the smart jobs to countries with loads of educated people who have an entrepreneurial spirit.

We lost the so-called dirty jobs, and now we're losing the jobs they told us we would keep. You can find some of them in a sleek new building in an ultramodern commercial and industrial park just outside the ancient Chinese city of Wuxi, 125 miles west of Shanghai. The Wuxi R&D Center is a principal research facility for Caterpillar Inc., the Peoria, Illinois–based maker of construction and mining equipment. Caterpillar's Wuxi research hub is a 10,000-square-foot LEED-certified facility that conducts research on a wide range of Caterpillar products. Its laboratories test new engines, materials, systems integration, and electronics. Opened in 2009, Caterpillar staffed Wuxi with five hundred engineers and support staff.

The R&D lab followed Caterpillar's major investment in manufacturing plants in China. Since 2007, when Caterpillar opened its first factory there, the company has been on a tear in the People's Republic. A Caterpillar plant in Xuzhou manufactures excavating machines, a plant in Suzhou turns out graders, a factory in Tongzhou produces large wheel loaders, a plant in Jiangsu province makes engines. All told, the company has seventeen manufacturing plants in China so far.

Just two years after opening the Wuxi R&D Center, Caterpillar announced a major expansion there to add more laboratories for fuel systems, electronics, cooling, rollover protection, and virtual reality. Caterpillar said the center also would have "extended design capabilities."

"China is the largest construction equipment market in the world, and Caterpillar continues to invest in China to help our Chinese customers succeed and to position Caterpillar for long-term leadership in China," said Caterpillar vice president and chief technology officer Tana Utley. "The Wuxi R&D center is enabling Caterpillar's product development success in China and other growth markets," Utley added.

The exodus of American plants offshore has become commonplace, but the flight of more and more high-value jobs to facilities such as the Caterpillar laboratory wasn't supposed to happen. Those were to be our jobs, the next stage in our development after we offloaded the low-skilled jobs. But things aren't working out according to plan. The Chinese government isn't content to just snag a plant of a Fortune 500 corporation; it wants some of the company's brainpower too. And American multinationals, lured by the prospect of cheap labor and higher profits, are giving the Chinese what they want.

In exchange for the right to build plants in China, corporations are agreeing to turn over proprietary technology. Soon the Chinese will make the products for themselves without the help of their American tutors. In some cases, engineering and design knowledge—some of it funded by U.S. taxpayers—will flow to the Chinese, allowing them to shortcut a development process that ordinarily takes generations. R&D centers in which U.S. companies develop new products in tandem with the Chinese are found in many locations in China today. Boeing has one, and so does DuPont. So do scores of other U.S. multinationals.

Eli Lilly, the Indiana-based global pharmaceutical giant, represents yet another step in the transfer of high-value jobs. The corporation has established with a Chinese company laboratories in Shanghai and Beijing that will develop new prescription drugs. Pharmaceutical researchers in the United States are among the more highly paid members of America's middle class. Without a doubt, more and more of these jobs will be flowing to China, India, and other developing nations.

As American policymakers continue to extol the benefits of free trade, the Chinese ignore the rhetoric and continue to build a self-sufficient economy the old-fashioned way—by protecting and enhancing its domestic industries. What need will China have to import much of anything from us once it has created all the basic industries? Meanwhile, the United States will become even more dependent on China as we send jobs and industries there.

None of this matters to multinational corporations and the Wall Street analysts who cheer them on. In exchange for short-term profits and hefty compensation, they are jeopardizing the country's future. They illustrate chillingly what Ralph Gomory, the longtime head of research at IBM, president-emeritus of the Alfred P. Sloan Foundation, and a longtime critic of U.S. trade policy, has warned about. As Gomory told a congressional committee in 2008:

> What is good for America's global corporations is no longer necessarily good for the American economy.
>
> We need to change this and better align the goals of corporations and the aspirations of the people of our country.

CHAPTER 9

RESTORING THE
AMERICAN DREAM

Over the last four decades, public policies driven by the economic elite have moved the nation even further away from the broad programs that helped create the world's largest middle class, to the point that much of that middle class is now imperiled. The economic system that once attempted to help the majority of its citizens has become one that favors the few.

Not everyone in the middle class who pursued the American dream expected to get rich. But there was a bedrock sense of optimism. Most people felt that life was good and might get better, that their years of dedication to a job would be followed by a livable, if not comfortable, retirement, and that the prospects for their children and the generations to follow would be better than their own.

Pam Sexton, a market researcher and engineer with two college degrees, described her version of the American dream like this: "The American dream is that you can work hard and be rewarded for your hard work. You'll be able to have a home and family and prosper and have medical care and not have to worry about expenses and bills. This is a country of opportunity." But Pam, along with thousands of others, lost her telecommunications job in 2009, and the dream died: "I feel like the last few years that's all disintegrated or evaporated." It is a refrain we've heard across the country.

The economic collapse after 2007 was responsible for much of the most recent damage to the middle class, but even when unemployment declines significantly and the economy improves, all the policies that have been eroding the middle class will still be in force.

A version of the middle class will survive. There will be jobs that pay well, and the people who get them will enjoy many of the benefits of their parents. But the size of the middle class is in jeopardy. In the past, it seemed that a broad band of opportunity was accessible to increasing numbers of people who worked hard and played by the rules. That has changed: the middle class is shrinking alarmingly, and there are fewer and fewer entry points.

What follows is a list of the bare minimum of steps that in our view must be taken to restore the vibrancy of middle America so that it is a realizable dream for most Americans, not just the lucky few. These measures would go some way toward achieving equity and prosperity for everyone.

REVISE THE TAX CODE

If you were one of the richest Americans in 1955, you paid on average about 51.2 percent of your income in federal taxes. If you were one of the richest Americans in 2007, your tax rate had plummeted to an average of 16.6 percent. Over that period, Congress systematically cut tax rates for the rich, allowed certain income to be excluded, and enabled the wealthy to funnel vast amounts of money through loopholes.

The justification for cutting tax bills was to stimulate the economy and create jobs. That hasn't happened; instead, tax cuts have given us a wealth gap greater than at any time since the late 1920s, when a similar chasm between the rich and everyone else foreshadowed the Great Depression.

Not only should we stop cutting taxes for the rich, but the very rich should pay more. Paying higher taxes wouldn't affect their lifestyle, and it would make our society as a whole more prosperous, which in the end benefits everyone, including the very rich. It also would dramatically reduce the federal deficit, which has soared in no small part because of tax cuts extended to the rich over the years.

Of all the economic challenges facing the middle class, the tax system should be the simplest to correct: what needs to be done is to reinstitute a series of tax rates that would apply largely to upper-income taxpayers. This would eliminate the situation that puts taxpayers who earn $388,000 a year in the same tax bracket as those who earn $50 million.

Most of the rich, of course, strenuously oppose paying higher taxes. Ever since the income tax was first levied, income tax foes have denounced any system that contains more than two or three rates as being too "complex." What they really mean is that, when there are more rates, the ruling class and their wealthiest friends have to pay more. Listen carefully to debates over the need to confine the number of rates to two or three to simplify the tax code. Keep in mind that a code with ten rates is every bit as simple as a code with two rates. Revising the code to add more rates would just mean the wealthy have to pay more of their fair share.

"Simplification" of the tax code has been a Trojan horse promoted by the rich and their allies for years; it's a concept that lures people into thinking that fewer rates would provide a more just system, when in fact it's just the opposite. U.S. congressman Paul Ryan, the House budget chairman, submitted a proposed budget in 2012 that he claimed would "simplify" the tax code by reducing the number of tax brackets and lowering the top rate on the wealthy to 25 percent. Nothing could be simpler—at least for the ruling class and their friends who would rake in the billions. And nothing could be more catastrophic for working people. And the rest of America.

The tax code is complex, but not because of the rates. In fact, much of the complexity stems from provisions—usually tax exclusions—that have been inserted to take care of those at the top. Dividend income was taxed the same as wages and salaries for many years until Congress lowered that rate in 2003. This complicated the tax code and put a costlier oversight burden on the IRS, but it was a huge gift to the wealthy. And it's a gift that would keep on giving if Congressman Ryan has his way. The tax proposal he floated in 2012 would eliminate federal income taxes entirely on dividend, interest, and capital gains income, a windfall of staggering proportions to the wealthy.

If Congress were serious about making the tax code simpler and fairer, what might it do? Why not create an individual tax system that requires an annual 1040 return of no more than a single sheet of paper? It would include all of your income and the sources of that income—wages, interest, dividends, rental income, what's referred to as capital gains and royalties. In short, every dollar of gross income from whatever source derived.

The sum of all that income then would be multiplied by your tax rate. No deductions for any purpose. No tax credits. No personal exemptions. There would be multiple rates, possibly as many as a dozen, running up to a top rate of 50 percent, which would be applied to all income over, say, $10 million. Multiple rates would ensure, as a matter of fairness, that people in totally different economic circumstances would not be lumped together in the same tax bracket, as has been the case since the highly-touted tax overhaul during President Reagan's era.

The task of salvaging a fair corporate tax code is complex, in no small part because the current code has been bought and paid for by the elites, the giant corporations, and the special interests. This code has the unfair and undesirable consequence of taxing most heavily and treating most unfairly those companies that operate entirely within the United States. These are the businesses that actually provide jobs for Americans—grocery stores, dry cleaners, tool and die shops, small clothing makers, construction companies, bus companies, theaters, manufacturers that employ anywhere from a few hundred people to several thousand—and have no dealings of any kind outside the country. For these businesses, which create jobs here, not abroad, there is no offshore tax haven or slick way to move money around the world. The only way to reform the corporate tax is to toss out the current code and replace it with a system that treats everyone the same. That's no small challenge. The system Congress has crafted taxes corporations at the same rate, but special deals inserted into the tax code by lawmakers beholden to corporations dramatically lower tax bills.

So maybe it's time to begin experimenting with new approaches. One possibility is a sales tax on all Wall Street transactions, everything from individual stocks to the latest exotic instruments. Even a modest levy—less than the rate most people pay in sales taxes—could generate hundreds of billions of dollars in revenue. Far-fetched? A financial transactions tax is under active consideration by the European Union. Another option: A gross receipts tax, which would make avoidance and evasion more difficult.

Lastly, it's impossible to talk about taxes without mentioning the one issue that has needlessly stirred panic among many seniors concerned about their Social Security—the national debt. Contrary to the frenzied claims advanced by Republicans—notably House Budget Committee Chairman Paul Ryan—along with private citizens who speak for the ruling class, the sky will remain where it is if the debt is not quickly eliminated. In truth, the budget deficit and debt issues are nothing more than a vehicle to continue tearing down the safety net of millions of Americans.

That's not to say we can continue adding to the debt in the reckless way we have over the last two decades. But the working poor and the middle class should not have to bear the burden of that debt through cuts in government programs as well as higher taxes. There is no legitimate reason to terminate programs that serve only the poor or working class. And there most decidedly is no good reason to even talk about cutting Social Security. It has not contributed a dollar to the debt. In fact, over the years, excess Social Security dollars have been used to pay for wars and ordinary programs and mask the size of the debt. The day will come when some action will be needed to bring Social Security taxes and payments into balance, but that is achievable.

Whatever decisions are made on taxes will go a long way toward either resolving or exacerbating the deficit and national debt. Over time, a carefully targeted tax system, combined with judicious spending cuts—like no more wars unless they are fully funded with a new tax—will reduce the debt and eventually eliminate it. There is absolutely no need for the irrational hysteria of the deficit hawks in and out of government.

MAKE FREE TRADE FAIR

The policies we have followed for half a century have failed. Under them, dozens of U.S. industries have been gutted by imports, and new industries that could offset some of the job losses haven't been given the support they need to help their products break through the obstacles to foreign markets.

A healthy national economy requires a balance of imports and exports. That's the principle followed by our major trading partners. But imports into the United States have been out of balance with exports ever since the 1970s as each year imports overwhelm exports and drive up the trade deficit. This deficit, now the world's largest, kills jobs. It urgently needs to be fixed; it is a much more pressing piece of business than the clueless ideological expansion of an idea—free trade—that may simply add to the instability of the U.S. economy. Instability benefits no one— except market speculators. It's time our trade policy was asked to serve the interests of all Americans—not just the markets and the people who control those markets. A good place to start would be to limit subsidized imports and insist that foreign nations lower their barriers to our goods. That would go a long way toward ending our massive trade deficit.

Barriers to U.S. companies are real. Every year the U.S. trade representative compiles a report on the ways in which foreign governments block imports of U.S. products, the *National Trade Estimate Report on Foreign Trade Barriers.* The 2011 version runs

382 pages and describes in detail how other nations discriminate against U.S. services and products. Here's a snapshot:

The European Union: After many years of negotiations, the European Union maintains "significant barriers" to U.S. products, "despite repeated efforts to resolve them."

Japan: "The U.S. Government has expressed concern with the overall lack of access to Japan's automotive market, as well as with specific aspects of Japan's regulatory system that limit the ability of U.S. automobile and related companies to expand business in the Japanese market."

China: "Many U.S. industries complain that they face significant nontariff barriers to trade. . . . These include regulations that set high thresholds for entry into service sectors . . . and the use of questionable . . . measures to control import volumes."

What's most troubling about the 2011 report is that it contains nothing new; every year the report reads the same as the year before. The types of barriers change, but the obstacles remain, with the same result—many of our products cannot be sold in other countries.

What can be done?

The most obvious solution is to enforce existing trade laws by taking action against governments that unfairly subsidize their own industries and undermine the jobs of U.S. workers. This could be accomplished in some cases only by imposing tariffs—perhaps even high tariffs. The very mention of tariffs infuriates free-traders and the ruling class. But the U.S. economy is in a battle for its survival. Our competitors will not safeguard our interests over their own. Nor will corporations whose wealth is held substantially outside U.S. jurisdiction. We have to take responsibility. But unless we are willing to enforce the law, other countries will continue to ignore U.S. pleas to open their markets to our products.

For years American manufacturing has suffered at the hands of economists from leading business schools who have downplayed its importance in the economy. This needs to change. The head of a Silicon Valley technology firm, Henry Nothhaft, argues that domestic manufacturing is essential not only because of the jobs and security it provides to workers, but also because it is crucial to innovation.

"R&D de-coupled from manufacturing eventually results in the loss of incremental innovation which occurs on the factory floor," Nothhaft has written. Because of corporate America's obsession with downsizing and short-term profits, he says, "we have gutted our ability to build the most advanced high-tech products of tomorrow." Similarly, Nothhaft says, "for every manufacturing job lost, ripple effects of job destruction and income erosion spread like a plague throughout the economy."

Relatively new companies like Google are often cited as classic examples of the entrepreneurial American venture that comes along in every era that injects life into the economy. But not every company can be, or should be, a Google. Our economy still runs on products that have been around for decades and are essential to the nation's well-being—its consumers and workers. As Ralph Gomory, the onetime head of research at IBM, told a congressionally-appointed study committee in 2011: "To prosper a country needs to make a range of good products and services, and then keep after them year after year, constantly learning and improving their capabilities to stay with or ahead of the competition." Those companies need congressional support quite as much as, if not more than, the multinational corporations. If they are to grow, they must find and develop markets abroad as well as domestically.

Though the nation has done little to alter the free-trade policies that have destroyed so many jobs, hopes began to rise recently that the long slide in manufacturing employment as a result of those policies might be over. For the first time in many years, factories were consistently adding jobs; 400,000 were added in 2010–2011. In his State of the Union address in 2012, President Obama singled out manufacturing for special mention: "We have a huge opportunity, at this moment, to bring manufacturing back. But we have to seize it."

It may be just another one of those economic mirages that have spurred false hopes over the years. But it would be a defining moment in rebuilding the middle class if the slide in manufacturing jobs were to be significantly reversed. At the very least, what we must do is halt the growth in the trade deficit—to stop the bleeding that has resulted from the carnage in lost plant jobs in recent decades, to ensure that the manufacturing sector that's left is stabilized and bolstered by a change in our trade policies. That alone would be a major victory.

INVEST IN AMERICA

There is only one player capable of offsetting the decline in private investment in this country that has resulted from U.S. corporations sending jobs and plants offshore and investing in other countries: the federal government.

Washington has the power to make an investment that would dramatically benefit the middle class as well as all other citizens. Instead, Washington is paralyzed. Intimidated by the deficit hawks who are funded by the ruling class, they decry any action that requires more federal spending. Contrary to what you hear and read in much of the media, in our view the nation should not be worried about federal spending right now. The federal deficit is an important, long-term problem, but unless we restore prosperity by creating more good-paying jobs, worries over the deficit will be moot.

One way for the government to create jobs would be to make a massive investment in infrastructure—not a make-work program, but a broad-based investment phased in over many years.

This would boost the economy by creating millions of jobs in construction, manufacturing, and other industries. This would be a wise investment even if the economy was in fine shape and unemployment was low, because the country's basic infrastructure is falling apart from years of neglect.

The American Society of Civil Engineers (ASCE) issues a periodic report on the state of the nation's bridges, highways, dams, rails, waterways, ports, water systems, and tunnels—all the components of our nation's infrastructure. Nearly all of these facilities are in such bad shape that they get no better than a D grade from the ASCE. "Delayed maintenance and chronic underfunding are contributors to the low grades in nearly every category," the ASCE concluded in its 2009 report. Just fixing current structural problems and upgrading those facilities would cost $2.2 trillion, the ASCE estimated. The deterioration is accelerating at such a pace that the ranking of the United States on infrastructure plunged from first in 2006 to sixteenth in 2011, according to the World Economic Forum.

Like so many other aspects of the economy described in this book, infrastructure investment is another casualty of the political dominance of the ruling class, whose private planes and gated residences lead them to think that infrastructure is less than essential to them. From 1950 to 1979, during a period when the United States funded broad-based public programs, its investment in transportation, water management, and electricity transmission grew at an average rate of 4 percent each year—about the same as the growth of the economy during that time. But from

1980 to 2007, when U.S. investment in infrastructure was scaled back to 2.3 percent, economic growth also fell, to an average annual rate of 2.9 percent, according to a 2009 study by the Political Economy Research Institute (PERI). "Faster public investment growth produces faster overall growth," concluded PERI.

In contrast, China and Japan, the chief competitors of the United States in Asia, are investing heavily in infrastructure—railroads, highways, Internet networks, ports, airports, and all the basic services that promote commerce and create jobs. Visitors to those nations are often stunned by the sophistication of the new technology that the Chinese and Japanese are pouring into their basic infrastructure. Visitors arriving at JFK before driving to New York City don't have quite the same sense of awe.

RETHINK TRAINING

The nation's federal training program for workers who lose their jobs to imports or offshoring is sorely in need of reform. Interviews with laid-off workers showed a pattern of frustration with the Trade Adjustment Assistance (TAA) offices in many states. Although workers were appreciative that the program existed, many reported that their caseworkers were overwhelmed with work, rarely if ever returned their calls, and sometimes weren't sure if they could even be of help. Others told of TAA caseworkers who were so overworked that they refused to give their last names, presumably to make sure they weren't contacted outside of work hours. Other workers who had been laid off complained that TAA was out of touch with reality.

Terri Steger was a systems analyst for AT&T and one of its contractors for thirty-five years in Milwaukee before her IT job and the jobs of her coworkers were shipped to India in 2009. She soon found herself in an orientation class sponsored by the local TAA office in Milwaukee to help her and others who had lost their jobs decide on their next career. Steger said that one of the federal officials suggested to the group that they consider information technology.

"We raised our hands and said, 'Wait a minute, you might want to rethink that, because we're all in information technology and our jobs are in India right now,'" she said.

An even greater shortcoming in U.S. training programs is the lack of well-funded, well-publicized, and highly respected apprenticeship programs. Such programs would give high school graduates who are unable to go to college, or whose skill sets are in other areas, a way to obtain training that would make them valuable to employers and enable them to earn a good living. The U.S. emphasis on college at the expense of apprenticeship programs has long been a complaint of many American industrialists, sociologists, and other experts. In other countries, notably Germany and Switzerland, apprenticeship programs are considered a fundamental part of secondary education and have been a major factor in the manufacturing success of those countries.

UPHOLD THE LAW

It sounds almost old-fashioned: to protect the middle class and all other Americans from the charlatans of Wall Street who served up the great housing meltdown, let's start enforcing the law. The triumph of the ruling class is so complete that there's no longer serious prosecution for violations of fraud and other statutes, which, if enforced, might discourage financial bandits in the future. If people end up in prison for committing a misdemeanor, surely they could go there for destroying the lives of working people.

Unless we do that, the story still playing out today across the United States will be repeated in some fashion in the years ahead when Wall Street cooks up its next great scheme. So far, more than 8 million homes are in some stage of foreclosure. Millions more are teetering on the edge. To hold down the number on the market, the government has authorized the bulldozing of empty houses.

As the housing market imploded and trillions of dollars in home equity vanished, millions of homeowners watched their most valuable asset disappear. In effect, that money was stolen by Wall Street with the touch of a keystroke. Two hedge fund managers alone made billions of dollars by betting the house of cards would collapse. So it wasn't as if no one saw what was happening. The equity that went up in smoke was money the middle class and the working poor were counting on to pay medical bills, fund college tuition for their children, help aging parents, or support their own retirement. All gone.

Despite the literally tens of thousands of illegal acts committed throughout the years of the great swindle, not one corporate executive or Wall Street titan has been charged with a crime. Any reasonably curious prosecutor, who was so inclined, could start at the bottom and work his or her way up the food chain, beginning with all the statements attesting to the value of a mortgage applicant's assets. It would have been rather easy since the paperwork was known laughingly across government, the banking industry, Wall Street, and the mortgage industry as "liar loans." The people who arranged the mortgages were rewarded with oversized bonuses. So, too, their bosses. The phony loans then were packaged into securities sold by Wall Street, which started the process all over by attesting that they were of prime quality. The securities were peddled to investors who were suckered by Wall Street's spiel. And on and on it went.

Law enforcement has been feeble; many prosecutors lack backbone, will, or imagination. This contributes to the pervasive attitude that for some the ordinary rules do not apply. Indeed, this is a pretty good definition of the ruling class: they can avoid the rules. Those who control the economy as well as the country implemented the doctrine of "too big to fail": select corporations would not be subject to bankruptcy rules but would be bailed out by the taxpayers. The likes of Goldman Sachs and Morgan Stanley would have to be rescued—by the little people. The principle also has been established that government bailout money can be used to pay executive bonuses.

The "too big to fail" doctrine helped trigger the largest economic collapse since the Great Depression, yet inexplicably Congress left the principle intact. Given the right circumstances, another unsuspecting generation will be blindsided by another crash. There's more. Congress bought into the idea that if select Wall Street firms and banks were too big to fail they also were too big to prosecute. Handing the moneyed a permanent "get out of jail free" card, Congress placed the ruling class as far above the laws of the land as they were above the laws of the market.

WILL THE MAJORITY RULE?

Most of the changes essential to restoring the American middle class require congressional support, but Congress has largely been on a thirty-year holiday from economic reality—at least as far as the middle class is concerned. Once in a while, however, even Congress has to come back to the people. Significant attempts to restore equity to the tax code by raising taxes on the wealthy will be met with cries of "class warfare," and any effort to temper the power and tax exemptions of U.S. multinational corporations that would limit their ability to invest outside the United States and send jobs abroad is certain to be met by a ferocious lobbying assault in Washington. Corporations also will argue that the goods they import made by cheap labor will provide lower-priced consumer items for sale that are good for our economy. But what kind of a society will we have if low prices are the ultimate measure of its worth? A society built on the economic principle that the lowest price is all that matters will be quite different from a society built on the principle that everyone who wants to work should receive a living wage. By putting the emphasis on the lowest possible price, we have sacrificed other values that create a healthy, productive society.

For all this to change, the people will have to prevail. Middle-class Americans, still the largest group of voters, must put their own economic survival above partisan loyalties and ask four simple questions of any candidate who wishes to represent them:

1. Will you support tax reform that restores fairness to personal and corporate tax rates?
2. Will you support U.S. manufacturing and other sectors of the economy by working for a more balanced trade policy?
3. Will you support government investment in essential infrastructure that helps business and creates jobs?
4. Will you help keep the benefits of U.S. innovation within the United States and work to prevent those benefits from being outsourced?

The choices we make in the candidates we elect and the programs and policies we support will set the direction of the country.

Many Americans are determined to restore rule by the majority. Last year, after we published some of our preliminary findings about the economic state of the middle class, many citizens wrote to us to offer their views. One man called for a "nonviolent revolution by the middle class." Another proposed a movement to turn everyone in Congress out of office. Still others, while acknowledging the gravity of the situation, also expressed hope, like this man from Illinois:

> Our market power is now so diminished, and our indebtedness so exorbitant, that we may have few levers left. But it is never too late to reorient our thinking and to correct a sustained injustice to our citizens.

What's at stake is not only the middle class, but the country itself. As the late U.S. Supreme Court justice Louis Brandeis once put it: "We can have concentrated wealth in the hands of a few or we can have democracy. But we cannot have both."

AFTERWORD TO THE
PAPERBACK EDITION

On May 28, 2013, the U.S. stock market hit an all-time high—15,409 on the Dow Jones—a peak not even achieved during the go-go years before the economic crash of 2008. The news media rejoiced: "Americans' 401(k)s are skyrocketing," blared ABC News. "What financial crisis?" asked a euphoric CNN Money.

A week later another statistic about the financial health of Americans surfaced, but it received little attention. Despite the financial markets' "recovery," average household wealth in the U.S. remained significantly less than it was in 2007, according to a study by the Federal Reserve Bank of St. Louis. The Fed calculated that average households had only recovered about 63 percent of what they had lost. In other words, Americans were one-third poorer than they were in 2007, despite the rising stock market. The Fed noted in a classic understatement, the recovery for these Americans—the vast majority of the country's citizens—"remains incomplete."

For all this talk throughout the 2012 election cycle by candidates from both parties about the urgent need to help the middle class, virtually nothing has been done to change policies that are impoverishing working Americans.

Public opinion polls before the November 2012 election showed that a significant majority of Americans supported higher taxes on the wealthy. But the White House–Congressional negotiations over taxes and spending that followed, though widely seen as a triumph for President Obama, ended in what can only be called a modest tax increase on the wealthy. How modest? As a result of the deal struck by the president and Congress, a couple with a taxable income of $500,000 will only pay a little more than $1,000 a year in additional income taxes.

The outcome of those negotiations signaled that it would be business as usual in Washington and reaffirmed the central theme of this book—that America is now ruled by an economic elite. The failure to achieve a significant tax increase on the one percent of very wealthy Americans shows how a minority can block a policy change favored by the majority. It forcefully demonstrates that America is no longer a democracy, but a plutocracy run by a few for their own benefit.

In the year since this book was first published, several other developments have brought into sharper focus some of the crucial issues explored in these pages.

The fiasco that followed the initial launch of Boeing's new passenger jet, the 787 Dreamliner, illustrates the potential pitfalls of outsourcing, a policy that more and more U.S. corporations have embraced to cut costs. The 787 is a revolutionary aircraft, and Boeing has staked a hefty bet on its success. But shortly after the jet began limited service late in 2012, all fifty models were grounded by the FAA after the lithium ion batteries that power the electrical system mysteriously began to overheat on two of the planes and ultimately failed within days of each other.

Despite the media's extensive coverage of the battery snafu, not enough attention was given to the fact that the 787's critical components were outsourced to foreign suppliers. An estimated 70 percent of the plane was outsourced—not just the batteries, but parts of the fuselage, wings, landing gear, rudder, and the electrical system as well. An investigation published in February 2013 in the *Seattle Times* concluded that the widespread problems with the 787's electrical system stemmed largely from outsourcing, much from Boeing's offshore supply chain.

This is an issue that goes well beyond the corporate pursuit of cheap labor. Outsourcing threatens the nation's ability to manufacture high-quality products for export. Once the technical issue with the batteries was apparently resolved, the 787 was once again cleared for flight, but the larger issue—that corporations are increasingly willing to sacrifice the quality of their products in favor of short-term profits—remains.

Boeing's Dreamliner was just another chapter in an all-too-familiar tale of the outsourcing of American jobs, but one potential glimmer of hope did appear on the job front last year—a wider recognition of the importance of manufacturing in the U.S. economy.

For many years, manufacturing jobs paid high wages and provided good benefits. They were the road to upward mobility for millions of working Americans. But from the 1970s onward, corporate actions and government trade and tax policies have systematically gutted the manufacturing sector. At the same time, corporate CEOs, politicians, and academic pundits have dismissed manufacturing as a relic of America's past. This is a view that helps large corporations justify the export of jobs to boost profits. And it supports the ivory tower theory shared by many economists, academics, and media commentators that the American workforce has been moving away from jobs dependent on brawn to those that rely on brain power.

But that view is finally changing. More and more Americans are realizing that manufacturing is an essential component of the nation's job mix. Even Walmart, the nation's largest employer—one that has done so much over the years to gut American manufacturing by compelling suppliers to produce products for the lowest possible prices—now claims to have had an epiphany on the subject of American manufacturing.

In a speech to the nation's retailers early in 2013, Bill Simon, Walmart's U.S. CEO, said that one of Walmart's new policies is "to support American manufacturing and to create more American manufacturing jobs." Simon acknowledged that retailers have encouraged investment in Asia for years, but said that now the equation is changing, and "if we can help create these [manufacturing] jobs here, it will make us proud as Americans." It is revealing that Walmart now says manufacturing jobs are again becoming essential—a tacit admission that service jobs (which the company creates) are not enough to sustain the economy. That has long been known, of course, as U.S. Bureau of Labor Statistics data shows: on average, manufacturing jobs pay nearly twice that of most service jobs.

Time will tell whether Walmart's position is more show than substance, but it's a reflection of how manufacturing jobs—so long denigrated as irrelevant by policymakers—are increasingly viewed as a critical component of the economy and crucial to the fortunes of the middle class.

The company that will show whether all this talk about the resurgence of American manufacturing is just ritual lip service by the nation's corporate elite or an actual stance regarding a sensitive domestic issue is Apple Inc. After widespread revelations about its export of good-paying middle-class jobs to sweatshops in China (where grueling working conditions drove some workers to suicide), Apple disclosed in 2013 that it would begin shifting some factory jobs back to the United States. Apple CEO Tim Cook said the company has committed $100 million to bringing one line of Mac computers back to the U.S. but did not say where they would be made or assembled.

Will all this talk of manufacturing turn into real action? We hope so, but not if a pattern long familiar in Washington reasserts itself.

In the past, when public opinion was outraged by practices of powerful interests that were destructive to middle-class jobs, those interests would often bow before public opinion and promise to change their ways. Then, as the pressure for reform subsided, the movement for change died with it. This has been the long-standing pattern for trade legislation in Congress: As anger over the unfair trading practices of foreign nations and multinational corporations has periodically erupted, Congress has adopted trade laws supposedly intended to level the playing field for global trade. But then Washington doesn't enforce the laws, and the job losses continue. The same thing could easily happen with manufacturing.

This time, though, there is a much wider recognition that off-shoring and outsourcing are hurting the middle class and that unless those forces are slowed or reversed, the erosion of wages and incomes will continue. *Manufacturing & Technology News*, one of the sharpest observers in this field, says that 2013 "might be the year" for change, pointing to the election of new senators who are more knowledgeable about trade and committed to find-ing ways to help middle-class America.

In addition to lost wages and a decline in incomes, the over-seas flight of manufacturing is causing concern about the U.S.'s ability to maintain its tradition of ingenuity and innovation. A 2013 report by the Aspen Institute and the Manufacturers Al-liance for Productivity and Innovation summed up the conse-quences if we continue to export manufacturing jobs:

When production goes overseas, innovation often follows. In many cases, designers and engineers must be in proxim-

ity to the process to ensure the steady flow of ideas. . . .
Wherever production takes place, R & D investment and
innovation follow. . . . Thus we lose not only our nation's
innovation capabilities, but the knowledge and network
spillovers that benefit the broader economy.

Even though more and more Americans subscribe to the view
that domestic manufacturing must be bolstered, the task of
changing public policy is formidable given the power of multinational corporations, foreign interests, free-trade ideologues,
and the financial power they wield in Washington. As long as
policy is still made with a dollar sign, it will be difficult to make
any changes. But to do any good, the U.S. must adopt a tougher
policy on trade and stop submitting to the will of the moneyed
elite. The outcome of the debate over manufacturing will have
ramifications far beyond factory jobs. As we show in this book,
the flight of work offshore has now moved well beyond traditional blue-collar occupations. White-collar jobs of educated
Americans are being shipped offshore too. Many of these service
occupations are the hope for America's future, but these are now
just as imperiled as blue-collar jobs were decades ago.

If the backlash over outsourcing and a renewed interest in
manufacturing offer a hint of hope for middle-class jobs, there
has been no change during the last year on one fundamental
issue: Washington remains in the grip of deficit hawks.

The economic elite have so successfully sold the misguided

notion that the U.S. budget deficit is the root of all current and future problems that there has been virtually no significant debate to challenge that theory. The staggering amount of misinformation on this topic, a good deal of it parroted by the media, has thwarted any meaningful public discussion of how we need to go forward as a nation.

Deficit hawks constantly warn the public that entitlements are bankrupting the country. To the average person with little direct knowledge of the nation's accounts, it might seem that 18-wheelers are backing up to loading docks at the U.S. Treasury and carting off tons of cash to local Social Security offices so they can send out the checks each month. Actually it's the other way around: Social Security runs a surplus. It collects more money than it needs to pay benefits and indirectly reduces the size of the budget deficit. Social Security has *nothing* to do with the nation's current budget deficit. But you would never know that from the TV reports, radio talk shows, or the frenzied accounts in newspapers and magazines that constantly warn about "runaway entitlements."

We as a country face painful decisions on Social Security and Medicare—how high to raise the eligibility age, how to rein in forever exploding health care costs, and what to do about the troubled disability fund of Social Security, which soon will be depleted. But what we desperately need to do now is to get the economy going again for millions of working Americans—not just to get them a paycheck, but to create good-paying jobs that provide a measure of security for middle-class families. That would do more to reduce the deficit than all of the meat-ax approaches of Washington combined.

To stimulate the economy, for both the short and long term, we need, among other actions, to make public investments in America that will pay dividends for years to come. Public investment spurs economic growth. Our investments in infrastructure—bridges, airports, and water systems—boost the middle class and benefit the nation as a whole. In the 1950s, for example, President Eisenhower marshaled broad bipartisan support to build the interstate highway system. That multibillion-dollar investment created millions of jobs, not just in construction, but in a host of other occupations as the federal money rippled through the economy.

We also need to invest in science, research, and technology—areas where there's no immediate payoff but that have the potential for significant long-term gain. Taking this long view is crucial to our future. This is not a radical idea: the U.S. has followed this approach with great success in the past. In the 1960s, the House of Representatives approved an appropriation for an obscure Defense Department agency called the Advanced Research Projects Agency (ARPA) that was experimenting with ways computers might talk to each other. ARPA's work helped create the Internet. What do you think the odds are of this happening today?

Although some deficit hawks no doubt honestly believe that debt will be the ruin of America, the fact is that many who advocate radical cuts in spending are only carrying water for the economic elite. There's a reason the rich constantly rail about the deficit: in their minds, the lower the deficit, the fewer taxes they will have to pay and the less money they will have to spend on public projects.

To make any of these changes—to reverse the tax, trade, and regulatory policies that are so harmful to the middle class—we must level the playing field for common citizens and give them a seat at the table alongside special interests that often own law-makers who are supposed to represent the people. The solution that is usually proposed is to limit the amount of money in poli-tics. What was driven home to us again and again at public meet-ings, radio shows, TV interviews, and book signings over the last year since this book was published is the near universal agreement among Americans that money is poisoning our democracy. Iron-ically, this is the one issue on which many on the left and right agree.

But to try to restrict the flow of money into politics poses many challenges. Previous efforts at the national level have failed, and even those who are appalled by the harmful impact of money in Washington hesitate to support constraints that might im-pinge on constitutional guarantees of free speech. To avoid that conflict, a constitutional amendment to limit money in politics is increasingly put forth as a solution. This movement was ener-gized by the U.S. Supreme Court's 2010 decision in *Citizens United v. Federal Election Commission*, which held that the First

Amendment prohibits the government from restricting campaign contributions—thereby opening the floodgates to unrestricted corporate cash in elections.

In our view, the answer is public financing of elections. We need to provide the financing to make sure a candidate who wants to enter public service can forgo special-interest dollars and still have a chance to win an election without selling his or her vote. How many of the lawmakers who bowed to pressure by National Rifle Association (NRA) dollars might have changed their vote on the assault-weapons ban in April 2013 if they knew they would have access to the same dollars and resources in their next campaign as an NRA-backed candidate?

Of course not all problems can be solved with public financing. Special interests would still have access to powerful, high-priced lobbyists, but their influence would be diminished if lawmakers knew their election-campaign war chests wouldn't depend on doing the bidding of the moneyed few. Several states and local jurisdictions have already adopted public campaign legislation that gives political newcomers a more solid footing, enabling them to challenge incumbents and make the electoral process less dependent on narrow interests.

Even if we as a nation are able to change our policies and return to a more balanced economy that benefits all citizens, we all know this won't happen overnight. But it's important to understand what some of the options might be and not to lose hope. All the great economic and social changes in American history, from Social Security to civil rights to women's rights, only came about after years—indeed decades—of work by those advocating change.

Restoring economic balance to the middle class will be a challenge of a similar magnitude. It may take years to achieve, but it must be accomplished if we are to save the American dream.

APPENDIX

Richest Pay Less

Effective Federal Tax Rate for Top 400 Families, 1955–2007

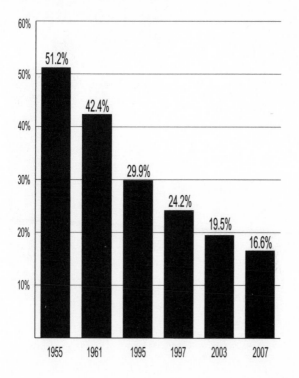

Sources: Top 400, 1955 and 1961: Janet McCubbin/Fritz Scheuren, Individual Income Tax Shares and Average Tax Rates, IRS, 1988 and 1989; 1995–2007: IRS, Statistics of Income, "The 400 Individual Income Tax Returns Reporting the Highest Adjusted Gross Incomes Each Year, 1992–2007." Research by Monica Arpino, Michael Lawson, Investigative Reporting Workshop
Graphic by Alissa Scheller, Investigative Reporting Workshop

The Real Deficit

U.S. global trade policies have wiped out millions of jobs and created a staggering trade deficit —the world's largest. Our main trading partners all run trade surpluses.

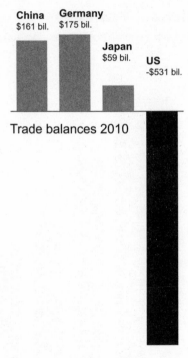

China
$161 bil.

Germany
$175 bil.

Japan
$59 bil.

US
-$531 bil.

Trade balances 2010

Source: World Trade Organization
Research by Monica Arpino, Michael Lawson, Investigative Reporting Workshop
Graphic by Alissa Scheller, Investigative Reporting Workshop

Corporations' Declining Share of the Tax Bill

Tax on corporate income as a percentage of GDP

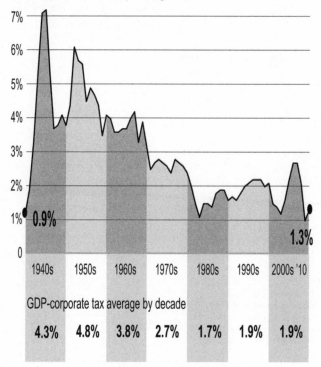

GDP-corporate tax average by decade

1940s	1950s	1960s	1970s	1980s	1990s	2000s '10
4.3%	4.8%	3.8%	2.7%	1.7%	1.9%	1.9%

Source: The President's Budget for Fiscal Year 2012
Research by Monica Arpino, Michael Lawson, Investigative Reporting Workshop
Graphic by Lisa Snider, Investigative Reporting Workshop

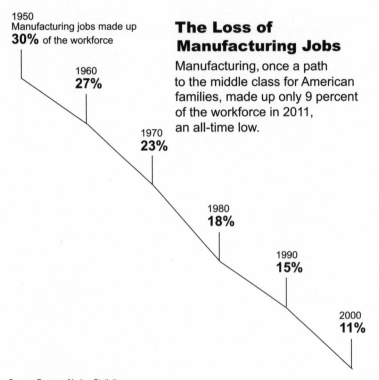

1950
Manufacturing jobs made up
30% of the workforce

1960
27%

1970
23%

1980
18%

1990
15%

2000
11%

The Loss of Manufacturing Jobs

Manufacturing, once a path to the middle class for American families, made up only 9 percent of the workforce in 2011, an all-time low.

Source: Bureau of Labor Statistics
Research by Monica Arpino, Michael
Lawson, Investigative Reporting Workshop
Graphic by Alissa Scheller, Investigative
Reporting Workshop

ACKNOWLEDGMENTS

We owe a deep debt of gratitude to all the men and women we interviewed who gave so willingly of their time. They welcomed us into their lives, invited us to sit with them around their kitchen tables, allowed us to visit them at their places of work, or talked to us for hours by phone to tell us their stories. They are the heart of this book, and their resilience and fortitude have reaffirmed our faith in the American people. To each one, we extend our heartfelt thanks.

This book would not have come to pass in its present form without the support, encouragement, and research assistance provided by the Investigative Reporting Workshop at the American University School of Communication in Washington, D.C. The Workshop is the creation of Charles Lewis, the preeminent figure in the ever-evolving world of nonprofit investigative journalism. We have known Chuck for many years, dating back to his days as founder and director of the Center for Public Integrity in Washington, and admire his courage, principles, and achievements. When we first discussed the idea of revisiting the story of what is happening to the American middle class, Chuck not only encouraged us to do so but suggested that we collaborate with the Workshop which could assist with research and provide a platform for our findings as well as for the work of others on the subject. Under Chuck's direction, the Workshop launched a multimedia research and reporting project called "What Went Wrong." It quickly became a research hub for information about the middle class and its website served as an invaluable vehicle for us and other writers to post the stories about working Americans. This fruitful collaboration with the researchers, writers, and producers at the Workshop produced a rich volume of journalism— more than forty multimedia stories alone in 2011—including work by us that ultimately became an important part of this book.

Many others at the Workshop deserve our thanks. Kat Aaron, the project manager for "What Went Wrong," helped to direct the research and brought her own deep knowledge, compassion, and expertise to the subjects we researched. Her professionalism, commitment, and exceptional contributions to the entire venture are deeply appreciated. Lynne Perri, the Workshop's managing editor, is as able, expert, and delightful a manager of a newsroom as you are likely to find—a wonderfully incisive editor and steadying influence. We would also like to thank senior editor Margaret Ebrahim for her excellent preliminary work in chiseling out from the vast themes we all followed a coherent story line that we hope will be the basis of a documentary based on this work. Senior editor Wendell Cochran, a longtime friend and fellow investigative reporter, provided ideas that were helpful in shaping the project. Thanks are also due to Barbara Schecter, the Workshop's able development director. We had the benefit of working with the Workshop's talented young staff, including Monica Arpino, Lydia Beyoud, Russ Choma, Jacob Fenton, Alissa Scheller, and Michael Lawson. Michael's sensitive interviews greatly enriched this story by providing a deeper understanding of the challenges that many Americans face today.

Also at American University, we want to express our thanks to Larry Kirkman, dean of the School of Communication, whose support and encouragement for this venture from the start is deeply appreciated.

Our remarkable collaboration with the Workshop would not have been possible were it not for the generous support of the Nathan Cummings Foundation, the Deer Creek Foundation, the Otto Haas Charitable Trust, the Public Welfare Foundation and the Wyncote Foundation.

Additional research for the project was provided by Allison Steele, whom we would like to thank for her thoughtful and incisive reporting.

At PublicAffairs, we have been fortunate to work with an extremely talented group of professionals who have given us all the encouragement and assistance any authors could ever expect: Peter Osnos, founder and editor-at-large, who enthusiastically supported this book from day one and offered wise counsel at every stage; publisher Susan Weinberg, whose support and encouragement were unstinting; and editor Clive Priddle for his outstanding editing, his intellectual curiosity, and his ability to draw out of us information we didn't even realize we had. We also want to thank three others at PublicAffairs who are emblematic of this deeply talented publishing house—Lisa Kaufman, Melissa Raymond, and Jaime Leifer.

We would also like to thank editors at the *Philadelphia Inquirer,* which copublished six articles we wrote for the Investigative Reporting Workshop: Stan Wischnowski and Rose Ciotta, who initiated the idea of copublishing with the Workshop, and Kevin Ferris, who shepherded the stories into print.

At the Wylie Agency, which has represented us for many years, we want to thank Jeffrey Posternak for his suggestions and his commitment to this book, as well as for his many courtesies and help through the years.

We are greatly thankful to Maxwell King, our former editor at the *Philadelphia Inquirer,* who was instrumental in helping to shape our 1991 series "America: What Went Wrong?" and who also urged us to write this book. Max gave a thoughtful, thorough reading of the first draft of this work and made his usual excellent suggestions, all the while offering his encouragement as we threaded our way through the thickets of trade and tax policy.

We would like to thank Martin Lobel, a Washington tax lawyer who for more than forty years has guided us through the labyrinth of the U.S. tax system, always with great patience and good humor.

And to Eileen Reynolds, who always asks the right questions.

Last, a special word of thanks to Nancy Steele, a superb editor who made important contributions to each stage of this project.

One final word: This book is another chapter in the continuation of a story we have been reporting and writing about for many years in newspapers, magazines, and books. Some of the individuals in this book have appeared in our previous work, but we have updated their stories to place them in the context of recent economic events. Staying in contact with some of them over the years has deepened our perspective about the plight of the middle class, which we have tried to convey in this book.

As always, whatever errors there may be, and we hope there are few, are solely our own.

A NOTE ON SOURCES

This book is based on interviews and public records and data from a wide variety of federal, state, and local agencies.

With few exceptions, the statistics used in this book were drawn from government and corporate sources. They include the U.S. Internal Revenue Service, the Bureau of Labor Statistics, the Federal Reserve Board, the *Annual Budget of the U.S. Government,* the *Economic Report of the President,* corporate filings with the U.S. Securities and Exchange Commission, the Congressional Budget Office, the Organization for Economic Cooperation and Development, the U.S. Department of Commerce, the U.S. State Department, the International Trade Administration, the Social Security Administration, and the U.S. Census Bureau.

Other sources of information at the national level included the U.S. International Trade Commission, the Employment and Training Administration of the U.S. Department of Labor, the Bureau of Economic Analysis, the United States Trade Representative, the Foreign Agents Registration Unit Public Office of the U.S. Department of Justice, the Center on Budget and Policy Priorities, the U.S. Department of Treasury, the Senate Records Office, the House Clerk's Office, the Government Accountability Office, the Employee Benefit Research Institute, the Pension Benefit Guaranty Corporation, the Interstate Commerce Commission, the Federal Trade Commission, the U.S. Department of Agriculture, the Inspector General's Office, *Public Papers of the Presidents,* the *Congressional Record,* and congressional hearings related to trade, taxes, and other economic issues spanning more than half a century.

We also collected information from many associations, nonprofit organizations, court jurisdictions, and local government agencies, including the Association for Manufacturing Technology, Footwear Industries of America, the Aerospace Industries Association, the Institute for Policy Studies, Good Jobs First, the Coalition for American Solar Manufacturing, the Offshoring Research Network, the American Manufacturing Trade Action Coalition, the National Consumer Law Center, the Center for Responsible Lending, the Community Reinvestment Association of North Carolina, the California Reinvestment Coalition, the Lee County (Florida) Circuit Court, the U.S. Bankruptcy Court for the Northern District of Texas, the Circuit Court of Van Buren County, Arkansas, and the Concord (California) Police Department.

As always, the libraries in many communities were vital in allowing us to access older records that haven't been digitized, including the Free Library of Philadelphia, the American University Library, the Wayne County Public Library of Wooster, Ohio, and the Bob and Wauneta Burkley Library and Resource Center of DeWitt, Nebraska.

We benefited from the work of others who have also studied the impact of economic measures affecting the middle class. We want to single out the 2010 report, "Shifting Responsibility—How 50 Years of Tax Cuts Benefited the Wealthiest Americans," by Chuck Collins, Allison Goldberg, and Sam Pizzigati. Published by Wealth for Common Good, a network of business leaders, high-income individuals, and others working to make the tax system fairer, "Shifting Responsibility" is a straightforward view of how tax policy has been hijacked by the rich.

While we used primary materials for the most part, some books and publications were invaluable. One of the most important books was *Manufacturing a Better Future for America* by Richard McCormack, Clyde Prestowitz, David Bourne, John Russo, Sherry Lee Linkon, Ron Hira, Irene Petrick, Peter Navarro, James Jacobs, and Michael Webber, published in 2009 by the Alliance for American Manufacturing. This is a compelling account of the systematic gutting of American manufacturing by American policymakers.

INDEX

A

Abramoff, Jack, 211
Accenture, 113, 114
AdAge, xix
Afghanistan, 143, 213
Aguiar, Jacob, 218
Aguiar, John, 215–218
Aguiar, Meghan, 218
Aguiar, Syrena, 215–218
Airline Deregulation Act, 197
airline industry. *See* deregulation
Albaugh, Jim, 66
Alcatel Data Networks, 56
Alfred P. Sloan Foundation, 244
Allen, Marc, 67
America: What Went Wrong?, ix, 11
America's Community Bankers, 192
American Airlines, 180–181,
    199–201
American Bankers Association, 192
American Bridge Company, 225
American Chung Nam, 62
American dream, ix, xx, 35, 36, 90,
    162, 218, 245, 246
American Graduate School of
    Business, Switzerland, 156
American Journalism Review, 167
American Manufacturing Trade
    Action Coalition (AMTAC),
    240
American Society of Civil Engineers
    (ASCE), 257
Americans for Prosperity, 29, 32, 33,
    35
Ames Research Group, 117

Anchor Hocking Glass Corp., 79
Andrews, Wright Jr., 211
Anheuser-Busch, 170
Apple Inc., xi, xii, xvi, 83–97, 110,
    135
Argentina, 114
Arison, Micky, 142
Arison, Shari, 142
Arison, Ted, 140–142
Armenia, 110
Association of Flight Attendants, 196
AT&T, 259
Art Basel Miami, 158
Atlanta, Georgia, 36, 42
Atlantic, The, 8, 160
Ave Maria, Florida, 164, 165
Aviation Industry Corporation of
    China (AVIC), 67, 68

B

Badman, Randy, 76–80
Bain Capital, 21, 23
Ballmer, Steve, 151
Bank of America, 100, 102, 146
Bank One Corporation, 174
Banking industry, 7, 12, 32, 111,
    160, 166, 191, 214, 218
    deregulation of, 192–193, 207–211
    escapes prosecution, 261–262
    low taxes of, 144–146
    promotes U.S. as tax haven,
        153–158
    See also Wall Street
Bankruptcy Abuse Prevention and
    Consumer Protection Act, 127

Donald L. Barlett and **James B. Steele** are the nation's most honored investigative reporting team, and authors of the *New York Times* bestseller *America: What Went Wrong?* This is their eighth book. They have worked together for more than forty years, first at the *Philadelphia Inquirer* (1971–1997), then at *Time* magazine (1997–2006), and at *Vanity Fair* since 2006. They are the only reporting team ever to have received two Pulitzer Prizes for newspaper reporting and two National Magazine Awards for magazine work. They live in Philadelphia.

PublicAffairs is a publishing house founded in 1997. It is a tribute to the standards, values, and flair of three persons who have served as mentors to countless reporters, writers, editors, and book people of all kinds, including me.

I. F. Stone, proprietor of *I. F. Stone's Weekly*, combined a commitment to the First Amendment with entrepreneurial zeal and reporting skill and became one of the great independent journalists in American history. At the age of eighty, Izzy published *The Trial of Socrates*, which was a national bestseller. He wrote the book after he taught himself ancient Greek.

Benjamin C. Bradlee was for nearly thirty years the charismatic editorial leader of *The Washington Post*. It was Ben who gave the *Post* the range and courage to pursue such historic issues as Watergate. He supported his reporters with a tenacity that made them fearless and it is no accident that so many became authors of influential, best-selling books.

Robert L. Bernstein, the chief executive of Random House for more than a quarter century, guided one of the nation's premier publishing houses. Bob was personally responsible for many books of political dissent and argument that challenged tyranny around the globe. He is also the founder and longtime chair of Human Rights Watch, one of the most respected human rights organizations in the world.

.   .   .

For fifty years, the banner of Public Affairs Press was carried by its owner Morris B. Schnapper, who published Gandhi, Nasser, Toynbee, Truman, and about 1,500 other authors. In 1983, Schnapper was described by *The Washington Post* as "a redoubtable gadfly." His legacy will endure in the books to come.

Peter Osnos, *Founder and Editor-at-Large*